Safe In The Secret Place

Twenty-Five Promises From Psalm 91

by
Camille Nehmsmann

David,
Thanks for all your help, prayers and encouragement in getting this book finished. You are a mighty man of God, and He has great things in store for you. Be blest!
Love In Christ,
Camille 5/5/01

Good News Ministries
Apollo, Pennsylvania

Col 1: 3+4 and 9-11 amplified

Scripture References

Unless otherwise noted, Scriptures are from the New King James Version (NKJ).

AMP   THE AMPLIFIED BIBLE, Old Testament, © 1965, 1987 by The Zondervan Corporation. The Amplified New Testament, © 1958, 1987 by the Lockman Foundation. Used by permission.

NIV   HOLY BIBLE, NEW INTERNATIONAL VERSION, © 1973, 1978, 1984 International Bible Society. Used by permission of Zondervan Bible Publishers.

NKJ   THE HOLY BIBLE, NEW KING JAMES VERSION, © 1982 by Thomas Nelson, Inc.

TLB   THE LIVING BIBLE, © 1971 by Tyndale House Publishers.

SAFE IN THE SECRET PLACE: TWENTY-FIVE PROMISES FROM PSALM 91
Copyright © 2001 Camille Nehmsmann

All rights reserved. No part of this publication may be reproduced, stored in a retrieval system, or transmitted in any form or by any means (electronic, mechanical, photocopy, recording, or any other) except for brief quotations in printed reviews—without the prior written permission of the author.

Cover artwork by Kathy Kinaitis.

Contact the author at:
Good News Ministries
301 Young Drive
Apollo, Pennsylvania 15613

Printed in the United States by Morris Publishing • 3212 East Highway 30
Kearney, NE 68847 • 1-800-650-7888

Dedication

*To my daughter,
Captain Katherine Nehmsmann Zeigler,
United States Air Force,
and to all the courageous,
dedicated men and women
who serve in the
American military*

*[God will give] strength to those who turn back
the battle at the gates.*

–Isaiah 28:6

Acknowledgments

My deepest thanks to:

My husband Lou, whose love, support and provision are invaluable;

David Bender, for countless hours spent editing this manuscript, and for his prayers and encouragement;

Kathy Kinaitis, who gave freely of her time and talent to create the cover for this book;

Mike, Nick and Linda Messina, who prayed daily for the completion of this book;

My sister Jean Chillseyzn, whose provision and enthusiasm helped this work continue;

Faithful prayer partners, whose encouragement helped me to persevere;

And especially to the Lord God Almighty, for His love, faithfulness, guidance, protection and salvation.

Effort has been made to accurately credit sources for the stories used here. However, since many have come from such sources as conversations with friends, radio broadcasts, sermons and news clippings, I am unable to identify every author.

Contents

Psalm 91 1

Introduction 3

Prologue 5

Chapter 1. Twenty-Five Promises 7

Chapter 2. First Things First 11

Chapter 3. The Shadow of the Almighty 15

Chapter 4. My Refuge and Fortress 19

Chapter 5. What Is the Snare of the Fowler? 23

Chapter 6. The Snare Is Broken and We Are Free 27

Chapter 7. Perilous Pestilence 31

Chapter 8. Under His Wings 37

Chapter 9. Fear Not! 41

Chapter 10. The Arrow That Flies by Day 47

Chapter 11. Victory Over Death 53

Chapter 12. When Everyone Around You Falls 61

Chapter 13. Your Place of Safety 67

Chapter 14. No Evil Shall Befall You 73

Chapter 15. Angels Will Guard You 79

Chapter 16. Heavenly Helpers 83
Chapter 17. Power Over Lions and Snakes 89
Chapter 18. Just a Coincidence? 95
Chapter 19. What's in a Name? 101
Chapter 20. The Great Escape 109
Chapter 21. Rescued and Honored 113
Chapter 22. Long Life and Salvation 121
Chapter 23. Never a Problem? 127
Chapter 24. A Friend of God 133
Chapter 25. Keys to the Secret Place 141
Prayers of Blessing 149
Appendix: Promises from Scripture 153
About the Author 159

Psalm 91

He who dwells in the secret place of the Most High
Shall abide under the shadow of the Almighty.
I will say of the Lord, "He is my refuge and my fortress;
My God, in Him will I trust."
Surely He shall deliver you from the snare of the fowler
And from the perilous pestilence.
He shall cover you with His feathers,
And under His wings you shall take refuge.
His truth shall be your shield and buckler.
You will not be afraid of the terror by night,
Nor of the arrow that flies by day,
Nor of the pestilence that walks in darkness,
Nor for the destruction that lays waste at noonday.
A thousand may fall at your side,
Ten thousand at your right hand;
But it shall not come near you.
Only with your eyes shall you look,
And see the reward of the wicked.
Because you have made the Lord, who is my refuge,
Even the Most High, your dwelling place,
No evil shall befall you,
Nor shall any plague come near your dwelling.
For He shall give His angels charge over you,
To keep you in all your ways.

In their hands they shall bear you up,
Lest you dash your foot against a stone.
You shall tread upon the lion and the cobra;
The young lion and the serpent you shall trample underfoot.
"Because he has set his love upon Me, therefore I will deliver him;
I will set him on high, because he has known My name.
He shall call upon Me and I will answer him;
I will be with him in trouble;
I will deliver him and honor him.
With long life I will satisfy him,
And show him My salvation."

—*New King James Version*

Introduction

All of us face challenging moments, when our own resources seem insufficient to overcome our circumstances. This careful study of Psalm 91 will impart confidence that God is willing and able to rescue those whose hearts are committed to Him. Your faith in His loving care will soar as you read true stories of Divine intervention in times of crisis.

A number of chapters in this book have evolved into miniature lessons, written for specific readers to whom the Holy Spirit wants to minister.

If a chapter speaks strongly to your heart, stop there and ponder what God might be saying to you. Read and meditate on the Scriptures given. Perhaps it's God's plan to set you free or encourage you in that area. Or the Lord may want you to pray for a person involved in the circumstances that chapter discusses.

May you clearly hear what the Holy Spirit will say as you read these pages.

–Camille Nehmsmann

Prologue

As the seasoned pilot flew his Cessna 180 from Texas to North Carolina, he had no idea he would soon experience a Divine encounter.

He and his traveling companion approached Ashville. The fog was so thick that the air traffic controller wouldn't let them land, suggesting they go on to Greenville instead. Since they had insufficient fuel to make it to Greenville, they got permission to make an emergency landing.

When the pilot lowered the plane, the radio sputtered: "Pull it up!"

To their horror the men realized they were about to land on the interstate.

The pilot pulled hard on the stick, and the aircraft barely missed a highway overpass.

"If you listen to me," the voice on the radio said calmly, "I'll show you how to get back in."

Then came a series of detailed instructions: "Turn left a little… Raise it up… Easy, easy… You're near the runway… Let it down—now."

The runway lights appeared through the fog, and the pilot and his companion landed safely.

First the men thanked God. Then they went in to thank the air traffic controller.

The controller on duty looked bewildered and said, "I don't understand. I lost contact with you right after I told you to make an emergency landing. Your radio sputtered, then you were gone…"

If it wasn't the air traffic controller, then whose voice so clearly directed the pilot to a safe landing? The men believe it was God's providential care that saved them.

This true story was printed in *Guideposts Magazine*, and is only one of many that illustrates God's safekeeping power in our lives.

One passage of Scripture details God's precious promises of protection over us. Turn the page and read with me twenty-five promises from Psalm 91…

Chapter 1

Twenty-Five Promises

The Book of Psalms is perhaps the most loved book in the Bible, depicting the life of the believer with its joys, sorrows, failure and victory.

Psalms is a compilation of 150 Hebrew songs or poems used for worship and private devotions. These poems were written over a long period of time, from 1000–300 BC. David penned many of them, but Moses, Asaph and others also contributed.

Though its authorship is uncertain, Psalm 91 is often attributed to Moses. Its lines may refer to events in the Book of Exodus as the Jews fled Egypt. The reference to plagues and thousands falling all around could reflect events in the first fourteen chapters.

Psalm 91 has enjoyed universal appeal through the ages as a poem of protection. It has encouraged many a missionary, weary traveler, battlefront warrior, as well as hosts of others who found themselves in dangerous circumstances.

As we study this psalm in detail, we'll see that protection is only one facet of its meaning. There are at least twenty-five promises contained in its lines, words of faith and hope for all of us.

Twenty-Five Promises Found in Psalm 91

"He who dwells in the secret place of the Most High...
1. Shall **abide under the shadow of the Almighty**.
    I will say of the Lord,
2. 'He is **my refuge and my fortress**;
3. My God, **in Him will I trust**.'
4. Surely He shall **deliver you from the snare of the fowler**
5. And **from the perilous pestilence**.
6. He shall **cover you with His feathers** and **under His wings you shall take refuge**.
7. **His truth shall be your shield and buckler**.
8. **You will not be afraid of the terror by night**,
9. Nor of the **arrow that flies by day**,
10. Nor of the **pestilence that walks in darkness**,
11. Nor for the **destruction that lays waste at noonday**.
    A thousand may fall at your side,
    Ten thousand at your right hand;
12. **But it shall not come near you**.
13. **Only with your eyes shall you look, And see the reward of the wicked**.
    Because you have made the Lord, who is my refuge, even the Most High, your dwelling place,
14. **No evil shall befall you**,

15. **Nor shall any plague come near your dwelling.**
16. For **He shall give His angels charge over you,** To keep you in all your ways.
17. **In their hands they shall bear you up,** Lest you dash your foot against a stone.
18. **You shall tread upon the lion and the cobra;** The young lion and the serpent you shall trample underfoot.

    'Because he has set his love upon Me,
19. **Therefore I will deliver him;**
20. **I will set him on high,** because he has known My name.
21. He shall call upon Me and **I will answer him;**
22. **I will be with him in trouble;**
23. **I will deliver him and honor him**
24. With **long life** I will satisfy him,
25. And show him My **salvation.**'"

—New King James Version

God gives a wonderful assurance to His children:

Jehovah Himself is caring for you! He is your defender. He protects you day and night. He keeps you from all evil, and preserves your life. He keeps His eye upon you as you come and go, and always guards you.
—Psalm 121:5–8 tlb

Chapter 2

First Things First

The salvation of the righteous comes from the Lord; he is their stronghold in time of trouble.
—*Psalm 37:39 NIV*

Salvation: God's saving grace; deliverance, safety

My husband and I made our way down dark and unfamiliar roads. It was midnight, and we were exhausted after a long trip. We could hardly wait to get to the motel and sink into bed.

When we arrived at the front desk, the clerk said there were no reservations for us. He also declared that no rooms were available anywhere in town. That weekend, Akron, Ohio, was hosting the annual Soap Box Derby, and every hotel was booked.

However, when we named the corporation that had sent us there, the clerk's tone changed. He affirmed that this company was one of the motel's best customers. He promised he would find us a room somewhere, somehow. And he did—not because of who we were, but because of whose name we had the right to use.

Likewise, to be beneficiaries of God's promises, we must belong to Him. We must accept Him as owner, boss and Lord of our lives.

When we give our hearts to Christ, we enter into a covenant or contract with Him, just as my husband had done with that Ohio company. Then, and only then, do we have the right to expect God to answer when we call. Only then are the promises of Psalm 91 guaranteed to us "by contract."

If you are not sure whether Jesus is your Lord and Savior, say a brief prayer like this one:

> Lord Jesus Christ, I admit that I am a sinner, and that You died and rose again to redeem me from my sins. Please forgive me. Come into my heart and be my Lord and Savior. Thank You, God, that You have heard my prayer, and I am now in Your kingdom. Help me to live the life You have chosen for me. Amen!

If you prayed that prayer from your heart, Jesus assures you that you are saved from hell. Accepting Jesus into your heart brings you into covenant with Him. This allows you to receive all the promises He has made in the Bible. Not only can you look forward to eternal life with Him in Heaven, you can experience His manifold blessings on the earth today.

Now you are ready to claim His blessings and promises. Together, let's walk through the doorway to wonderful revelations from Psalm 91.

> "If you remain [abide] in me and my words remain in you, ask whatever you wish, and it will be given you."
> –*JOHN 15:7 NIV*

"God so loved the world that He gave His one and only Son, so whoever believes in Him may not be lost, but have eternal life" (John 3:16). Not "everyone who achieves," not "everyone who succeeds," not "everyone who agrees," but "everyone who believes."

—Max Lucado

Chapter 3

The Shadow of the Almighty

> He who dwells in the secret place of the Most High shall remain stable and fixed under the shadow of the Almighty [Whose power no foe can withstand].
> –*Psalm 91:1* AMP

Shadow has the connotation (in the original language) of hovering over, protecting, defending, sheltering.

When Cherie was a child, her father always deadbolted the doors at night. He hung the key inside on a nail above the back door.

One night when she was about six years old, Cherie was awakened by a crash of thunder. When she saw smoke and flames, she knew the house was on fire. She tried to reach her parents' room, but the flames prevented her.

Cherie ran down the hallway toward her only escape, the back door. Fear gripped her when she realized the door would be locked. And she was not tall enough to reach the key.

Yet peace came over her when she felt a strong hand gently grip hers and, through the smoke and heat, lead her to safety out the back door. Her parents and siblings were outside, all accounted for and unharmed.

Imagine Cherie's amazement when her father ran up and told her he had tried to reach her through the flames but was unable. It was not he who had taken her hand, nor had he unlocked the back door.

To this day Cherie thanks the One who led her through the dark.

> You have hedged me behind and before, and laid your hand upon me... Your hand shall lead me, and Your right hand shall hold me.
> —PSALM 139:5,10

This book relates many stories of how our loving, protecting, Almighty God has rescued and encouraged people in various places and circumstances. We can enjoy these same benefits if we meet the requirements. Psalm 91 gives two conditions for receiving all its promises: We must abide in the Lord (verse 1), and we must set our love upon Him (verse 14).

The secret place (verse 1) is where we find the presence of the Lord. We can meet Him in a place set aside for daily fellowship, such as a prayer room, "prayer chair," or even our kitchen table (see Chapter 25). The spiritual connotation here, however, is remaining in God's presence on a continual basis. The person who dwells or abides in God does not run in and out, but remains in the presence of the Almighty. As we pursue the Lord we will find ourselves in His presence nearly all the time, no matter what else we are doing. While we are at work, at home, even traveling, we will sense that He is with us.

To be "under the shadow of" denotes:

Protection... God hovers over us to shield and shelter us from harm.

> In the shadow of your wings I will take refuge, and be confident until these calamities and destructive storms are passed.
> *—PSALM 57:1b AMP*

Power... When Mary was told by an angelic visitor that she was to be the mother of Jesus, she asked how this was possible since she was a virgin. The angel declared it would happen when the power of the Most High overshadowed her (see Luke 1:35).

A place of shade... which is cooling and refreshing. Another way of looking at it is that God will keep us cool in the heat of battle (see Psalm 121:5).

A place where we can rest... and even stop to enjoy good things and happy moments. With today's hectic pace, that is good news.

> You have been my help, and in the shadow of Your wings I will rejoice.
> *—PSALM 63:7*

"Almighty" literally means the All Sufficient One, unconquerable, the God who has more than enough power to meet our needs. Therefore, as we abide in the Lord, we are protected by God the Almighty, who has the strength and ability to preserve us from harm.

God loves us even more than an earthly father loves his children. If my natural father would let nothing harm me, think how much more secure I am under the shadow of my Heavenly Dad! Even if our earthly father was not the protector we needed, or was absent, God promises that He himself will take on that role.

> Although my father and my mother have forsaken me,
> yet the Lord will take me up [adopt me as His child].
> —PSALM 27:10 AMP

A report that captured headlines for months related the story of Elian Gonzales, a five-year-old Cuban boy. He, his mother and several others were in a boat in the Atlantic Ocean. They were fleeing from Cuba to the United States. The boat capsized, and nearly all aboard perished except Elian and one other.

For forty-eight hours, Elian was adrift in an innertube, alone. What are the chances of a five-year-old, clinging to an innertube, surviving the shark-infested waters of the Atlantic for two days and nights?

After fishermen rescued him, the boy said he was kept afloat by what he described as "dolphins." Whenever he grew weary and let go of the innertube, he said the dolphins swam under him and pushed him up again. Perhaps they kept circling sharks at bay as well. These sea creatures were his guardians and companions during that long ordeal. Even skeptics are amazed at this story of protection.

> The eternal God is your refuge, and underneath are the everlasting arms.
> —DEUTERONOMY 33:27a

Chapter 4

My Refuge and Fortress

I will say of the Lord, "He is my Refuge and my Fortress; my God; on Him I lean and rely; and in Him I [confidently] trust."
−PSALM 91:2 AMP

Refuge: A place providing protection or shelter. A source of help, relief, or comfort in times of trouble.

Most of us remember stories of the American Old West, where pioneers would run into a military fort for protection from their enemies. They were not only safe from enemy attacks, but were provided with food, shelter and other necessities of life. They took comfort in knowing they were not alone in the wilderness, on their own in times of danger.

In the fortress of God's protection, the Lord shields, comforts and even supplies material needs when required. Perhaps a day may come when we have little or no food and must rely solely on God's provision.

In Scripture, God many times supplied food for hungry people. God miraculously provided manna for the Jews as they wandered in the desert (see Exodus 16:15).

The Gospels relate how Jesus multiplied fish and a few loaves of bread to feed a hungry crowd (see Matthew 14:17–21).

I was told the story of a missionary in China forced to remain in her home for many days because an unexpected revolution made travel unsafe. She was without food and prayed to God for provision.

The same day a stray cat came to her door, wanting to come in. Each morning it begged to be let out. A little later the cat would return with a freshly caught fish in its mouth that it would lay at her feet. This continued daily until it was once again safe for the woman to go out to market. The cat disappeared the day the revolution ended and was never seen again.

> And my God shall supply all your need according to His riches in glory by Christ Jesus.
> – *Philippians 4:19*

God meets all the criteria to be our refuge and fortress: He is strong, yet tender enough to provide comfort when we need it. In *Him* will we trust, not in our possessions, job, spouse or friends. Those others are beneficial, given by the Lord to bless us. But they are not our final security.

A few years ago I was concerned about trouble that might arise while driving. I thought a cellular car phone would prove helpful. Although it is beneficial, the batteries wear out, and sometimes I drive out of range of a phone tower.

God's batteries, however, never run down and He is always within calling range. In fact, He has an 800 number—free and available twenty-four hours a day!

Billy Graham tells a wonderful story in his book *Angels: God's Secret Agents*.[1] It illustrates God's providential care over His beloved, even in the remotest parts of the earth.

Reverend Graham was visiting American troops during the Korean War and was told of a small group of Marines in the first division who had been trapped up north. The temperature there was twenty degrees below zero. Not only were the soldiers in danger of freezing to death, but they had had nothing to eat for six days. Their only hope for survival seemed to be to surrender to the Chinese.

But one of the Americans, a Christian, spoke aloud certain verses of Scripture and taught his comrades to sing praise songs to God.

Following this a wild boar came crashing toward them. One of the men raised his rifle to shoot it, but before he could fire, the boar inexplicably stopped and dropped dead in its tracks. They feasted on roast pig that night and were physically and mentally strengthened.

The next morning at sunrise they heard another noise and expected enemy troops. Instead they found themselves face to face with a South Korean who said, in English, that he would show them the way to safety. He led them through forests and mountains right to American lines. When they looked up to thank him, he had disappeared!

For the eyes of the Lord range throughout the earth to strengthen those whose hearts are fully committed to Him.
—2 Chronicles 16:9 NIV

Whether we need comfort, shelter, provision or protection, we can confidently rely on God to supply whatever is required for the moment.

The Lord is my rock and my fortress and my deliverer; The God of my strength, in whom I will trust; my shield... my stronghold and my refuge.
—2 Samuel 22:2–3

Endnotes:

1 Billy Graham, *Angels: God's Secret Agents*, p. 169.

Chapter 5

What Is the Snare of the Fowler?

Surely He shall deliver you from the snare of the fowler and from the perilous pestilence.
—PSALM 91:3

Snare: a trapping device, often used to catch birds

When Psalm 91 was written, people understood that the snare of the fowler was a cleverly disguised trap designed to entangle the unwary bird. Snares were subtle devices, shrewdly designed to look appealing to lure the bird. When the hapless creature went for the bait, a lid would drop over him and he was doomed.

The devil's pitfalls are like this. How many times have we fallen for things that looked good but turned out to be bad? The devil's snares can include people and places that aren't good for us. They can be books, movies and television shows that leave strong impressions that linger in our minds. We can be deceived by false teachings, promises and expectations. We can even be lured by the prospects of fame and fortune.

If we abide in the Lord we will be delivered from the devil's subtle traps. If we are safe in the fortress, the deceiver can't get at us. The Lord can manifest His protection a number of ways. God may speak caution to our hearts, arrange circumstances to prevent disaster, or send a message through another person or through a Bible verse.

Sometimes God intervenes in unusual ways—even if we have not yet committed our lives to Christ. Here is an example of just that.

A young woman loaded her handgun, preparing to rob a convenience store. As she left her house, a strong audible voice said, "Take the bullets out of the gun."

She looked around but saw no one, so went on her way, assuming the voice had been only her imagination.

Again the voice commanded, "Take the bullets out of the gun!"

It came with such authority that she emptied the gun, yet proceeded to rob the store.

When the clerk did not obey her orders quickly enough, she pointed the gun at his head and pulled the trigger repeatedly. Fortunately, there were no bullets in the gun. The woman was soon arrested, prosecuted for robbery and spent time in prison.

While incarcerated, the woman was introduced to the Lord Jesus Christ and received Him into her life. She served her sentence and, after her release, became a strong witness and worker for Christ. Her life turned around completely.

She knows full well that if it hadn't been for the mysterious command to remove the bullets from her weapon she would have killed the store clerk and been imprisoned for the rest of her life. Both she and the store clerk are very thankful for Divine intervention!

> Are not all angels ministering spirits sent to serve those who *will* inherit salvation?
> –HEBREWS 1:14 NIV

God wants to direct us, warn us about and rescue us from the devil's snares. Listen to that still small voice within you. As you communicate with the Lord regularly, abiding in the secret place, you'll learn to recognize the voice of God within you, guiding and teaching you.

> I [God] will instruct you and teach you in the way you should go; I will counsel you and watch over you.
> –PSALM 32:8 NIV

Chapter 6

The Snare Is Broken and We Are Free

Surely He will deliver you from the snare of the fowler.
—*PSALM 91:3a*

From: out of the possession or control of

Being saved from the snare of the fowler includes two concepts:
1. God's guidance will prevent you from falling into the trap, as in the preceding story about the young woman who robbed a convenience store.
2. If you have been ensnared, God will deliver you out of the trap.

Most of us have strayed off the path of righteousness on occasion. Even then, we can often recall God's protection despite our foolishness. This is not a license to sin, and we often suffer the earthly consequences of transgression. Yet Scripture tells us that God remains faithful even when we do not (see 2 Timothy 2:13).

Often we cannot see the trap laid for us by the devil. The Bible says: "The proud have *hid* a snare for me"

(Psalm 140:5), and "Surely in vain the net is spread in the sight of the bird" (Proverbs 1:17).

If a bird sees the snare he will avoid it. Likewise, the devil usually will not set a trap you can see. Rather, he devises a cunning method that will catch you unaware.

Perhaps you once flew free, but are now ensnared in the net of sin through the devil's cunning. Some of the traps he lays include pornography, drugs, fornication, stealing, lying, cheating and being involved in wrong relationships.

God can set you free right now! Call on His name: "Our help is in the name of the Lord" (see Psalm 124:8). Tell Him you are sorry (repent, turn around), and He immediately will forgive you.

The restoration process can begin this very moment!

> We are like a bird escaped from the snare of the fowler; the snare is broken and we have escaped!
> *–PSALM 124:7 AMP*

Moses, David, Peter and other heroes of Scripture all had moments of yielding to temptation, yet God forgave, restored and raised them up to be mighty men in His kingdom. It may take time and discipline, but you are not alone—God is with you to deliver you. As you call on His name, repent and persevere in obedience, He will certainly free and restore you.

A contemporary man whose potential was almost lost is Stephen Hill. He is a well known evangelist instrumental in the revival at Brownsville Assembly of God in Pensacola, Florida. Steve tells how he was in bondage to alcohol and drugs, wasting his life.[1] He was willing to commit crime to support his addictions. "What I really wanted to do," Steve says, "was drink myself into oblivion." Several of his young friends died of drug overdoses, auto accidents or were murdered.

Yet God rescued Steve through persistent, believing prayers on his behalf. In 1975, at the urging of a Lutheran minister, Hill cried out to Jesus. He suddenly felt "peace like I never felt before" flood his body. Hill says, "Jesus transformed my heart. I was clean, forgiven, and alive again!"

Hundreds of thousands of souls have surrendered their lives to Christ as the Holy Spirit works through powerful anointed preaching by Reverend Steve Hill.

If you have cried out to God to set you free, today is the day of your liberation! It's a brand new beginning and, from this moment on, you begin the journey to fulfill your God-given potential, to become all you can be in Christ! Don't go by what your eyes see or what negative emotions might tell you.

Last year a large tree in the woods on our property was blown down by the wind, uprooted and cut off from any source of life. Yet there continued to be green leaves on that tree for quite a while. An observer might have thought the tree was still alive, but because it was cut off at the roots, it eventually died.

So too, temptation to walk that old path, revisit that old sin, may seem to pursue you for a time. But if you have spiritually uprooted that thing, continue to *stand firm* against it with God's help. Be assured that it is dead. *Remain steadfast, and soon you will see that you are free indeed.* God has a great purpose for your life!

> For I know the thoughts and plans I have for you, says the Lord, thoughts and plans for welfare and peace, and not for evil, to give you hope in your final outcome. Then you will call upon Me, and you will come and pray to Me, and I will hear and heed you.
> —*JEREMIAH 29:11–12* AMP

Endnotes:

1 *Charisma*, Strang Communications, Lake Mary, Florida, May, 1999, p. 19.

Chapter 7

Perilous Pestilence

[God will deliver you] from the perilous pestilence.
−*PSALM 91:3b*

Pestilence: a plague, deadly disease; a series of attacks that come like a plague.

Swarms of locusts blackened the sky. They descended and devoured every plant in sight. This disaster came on the heels of other plagues: flies, diseased livestock, boils and hail.

Then thick darkness covered Egypt for three days. Yet the Bible says that during this time and in this same place, "all the children of Israel had light in their dwellings" (see Exodus 10:23).

The final crushing blow occurred when the firstborn of every living thing died—except those belonging to the Jews. God's people experienced none of these plagues, though they lived right in the midst of them.

The Israelites were surrounded by disaster on all sides and could easily have succumbed to terror, but they had confidence in God's power to protect them. They had a covenant relationship with Him, and as long as they kept their part of the agreement, they were kept safe.

Centuries later, another person spent her life ministering to the downtrodden, even those with horrible diseases such as leprosy and AIDS. Yet she died at the age of 87 from heart disease. Mother Theresa was surrounded by plagues on all sides, yet was preserved from catching these diseases.

Consider, too, the story of Charles Spurgeon, a well known preacher in nineteenth-century Britain. The words of Psalm 91 comforted him during a difficult time in his life.

In 1854, at about age twenty, he was called to pastor a church in London. This was during a serious cholera epidemic. The fatality rate was so high that Spurgeon conducted funerals for victims almost daily.

He became weary and discouraged about the scope of the plague, trying to comfort the grieving, and mourning the loss of so many friends. Spurgeon felt it was only a matter of time before he contracted the deadly disease because of close contact with so many who were dying. He was sinking in both body and spirit.

One day as he returned from conducting yet another funeral, a flyer in a shop window caught his eye. It contained these words from Psalm 91: "You will not fear the terror of night… nor the pestilence that stalks in darkness, nor the plague that destroys at midday. A thousand may fall at your side, ten thousand at your right hand, but it will not come near you" (Psalm 91:5–7 NIV).

The impact of these words was dramatic. Spurgeon wrote that he soon felt secure, refreshed, and had a calm, peaceful spirit. He had no fear of evil and suffered no harm. Not only was his health preserved during that epidemic, but he lived a long and fruitful life. Spurgeon went on to become an extremely successful preacher whose sermons filled over fifty volumes and were translated into several languages.

In the same way, we can expect to be protected from pestilence when we walk in obedience to the Lord. While caution and common sense are required, fear should not be found in the hearts of those who are in a covenant relationship with God. If we obey Him, He will safeguard us.

> For you have delivered my life from death, my eyes from tears, and my feet from stumbling and falling. I will walk before the Lord in the land of the living.
> *—PSALM 116:8–9 AMP*

Psalm 91:3 also promises help during a series of attacks. How often have you been hit with one thing after another and wondered how you would ever get through it all?

Recently my friend Deborah Zimm told me how her father went through a series of life threatening situations as a young man, yet lived to a ripe old age. Peter Crawford was a navigator in the United States Army Airforce during World War II. He faced danger nearly every day while stationed in Europe.

On one flight his plane was shot down over Normandy, France. At that time, the area was constantly patrolled by German troops. The young American bailed out. The rest of the crew, including the pilot, were all killed.

Crawford injured his leg in the jump, but managed to drag himself across the field toward a farm. A French school teacher found Peter and quickly carried him to a neighbor's barn. The Nazis had seen his parachute descend to earth and were searching for him, so the rescuer hid Peter under a pile of hay.

The Germans searched the barn thoroughly and repeatedly thrust their bayonets into the haystack where Crawford hid, coming within an inch of his body! Finding nothing, they finally left.

Peter still had a long way to go to get back to his group, and his wounded leg needed care. Eventually the young soldier was reunited with fellow American troops, where he received proper medical care. He went home after his tour of duty and lived a long fruitful life.

Back home in South Carolina his godly grandmother prayed frequently for twenty-two-year-old Peter while he was overseas. Although the young American had not yet committed his life to Christ, he would often talk to God, whom he referred to as "my Friend." Deborah is very thankful for Divine intervention in her dad's life, knowing she never would have been born had not the hand of God rescued her father that afternoon in France.

> Fear not, for I have redeemed you; I have called you by your name; you are Mine. When you pass through the waters, I will be with you; and through the rivers they shall not overflow you. When you walk through the fire, you shall not be burned, nor shall the flame scorch you. For I am the Lord your God…
>
> *–Isaiah 43:1b–3*

He Leadeth Me

In pastures green? Not always.
Sometimes He who knoweth best,
In kindness leadeth me
In many ways where heavy shadows be.
Out of the sunshine into the darkest night.
I oft would faint with sorrow and affright,
Only for this—I know He holds my hand.
So whether in the green or desert land,
I trust, though I may not understand.

And by still waters? No, not always so;
Oftimes the heavy tempests round me blow.
And o'er my soul the waters and billows go,
But when the storms beat loudest and I cry
Aloud for help, the Master standeth by
And whispers to my soul, "Lo, it is I."
Above the tempest wild I hear Him say,
"Beyond this darkness lies a perfect day.
In every path of thine I lead the way."

—Rev. John F. Chaplain

Chapter 8

Under His Wings

[Then] He will cover you with His pinions, and under His wings shall you trust and find refuge; His truth and faithfulness are a shield and buckler.
—*Psalm 91:4 AMP*

Shield: *noun:* an article of protective armor; *verb:* to protect, preserve, guard, cover, conceal

Buckler: a small round shield used to protect against blows to the body

Being covered with feathers gives a picture of gentle protection. When danger threatens or it's time to sleep, a mother hen tucks her chicks under her wings, which are covered with soft down. Trust allows the babies to feel secure there.

Being under God's wings gives the idea of a safe place, but there is also the connotation of comfort, of shutting the world out. It can bring to mind sinking into a down-filled mattress when one is weary or overwhelmed.

Mike and Nick Messina are two youngsters who, along with their mom Linda, prayed daily for the successful completion of this book. They sent me the following story, which was reportedly published in *National Geographic Magazine.*

After a forest fire in Yellowstone National Park, rangers toured the burned area to assess damage. They found a bird literally petrified in ashes, perched statuesquely on the ground at the base of a tree. Somewhat sickened by the eerie sight, one ranger knocked over the bird with a stick. When he gently struck it, three tiny chicks scurried out from under their dead mother's wings.

The loving mother, aware of impending danger, gathered the chicks under her wings for protection. She could have fled for her own safety, but refused to abandon her little ones.

Not only does this give a perfect picture of verse 4, it also reminds us that Jesus Christ died to protect us from eternal damnation. Well aware of the horrific death that lay before Him, He could have fled. Instead, He chose to die, so that we might live!

Our Shield and Buckler

In contrast to the gentle wings and feathers, shield and buckler are strong military terms that connote protection from arrows and fiery darts of the enemy in warfare. The shield was a large device that covered the soldier from head to toe, while a buckler was thought to be a smaller round piece of armor that was worn on the arm.

Scripture assures us that God's truth and faithfulness are part of His very nature. The Lord promises that He

Himself is our shield. Anything that would harm us has to pass through Him, and He is a formidable foe to our enemies! The Lord says, "Do not be afraid… I am your shield…" (Genesis 15:1).

Pastor Jack Hayford told the following story about Fred, a missionary friend of his.[1] It illustrates God's power to shield us in a time of mortal danger.

Fred was invited to a third world country to share the Gospel. To get to the village that invited them, his team had to travel through dangerous territory near a hostile community. Men had been martyred trying to reach that village. Because of dense jungle growth, the missionaries were forced to travel on a path fairly close to the hostile community; there was no other way to go.

Somehow the militant villagers were alerted to their presence, and Fred's group could hear the approach of those who sought to kill them. There was no other path for the preachers to take, no place of safety. It looked hopeless.

Suddenly a man appeared on the road before them and said, "Listen to me, and do exactly what I tell you. Stand with your back against the side of the overgrowth."

They followed his orders precisely, and the man reached out and spread his arms across the small group of men as they flattened themselves against the jungle brush. It was dusk when the soldiers, armed with guns, came right up to them—anyone could see the military men. Astonishingly, the soldiers didn't see Fred's group.

One soldier shone a flashlight right in Fred's face and said, "I think someone is here." But he looked right past Fred, seeming almost to look through him.

After a few minutes of searching, the hostile villagers left. That mysterious stranger who aided the missionaries stepped away from Fred and said it was now safe to continue on their journey. When they turned to thank him, the man was gone!

Whether we need the comfort of a quiet place to rest, gentle protection, or a militant defense against demonic forces out to destroy us, God promises to provide exactly what we require on each occasion.

> Lord... many are they who rise up against me! ... But You, O Lord, are a shield for me, my glory, and the lifter of my head.
> —PSALM 3:1,3 AMP

Endnotes:

1 Jack Hayford, Living Way Ministries, Van Nuys, CA. From a radio broadcast.

Chapter 9

Fear Not!

You shall not be afraid of the terror by night, nor of the arrow that flies by day.
—*Psalm 91:5*

Fear: a feeling of alarm or disquiet caused by the expectation of disaster; terror, dread, apprehension

It was a tough act to follow. The previous leader had a following of millions. Miracles had even happened on his watch. His death was mourned by a whole nation, and now Joshua was to take Moses' place and assume command. His orders were to lead millions of people safely out of the desert into a land belonging to fierce enemies, even giants.

Yet God had promised victory, so Joshua set about leading the nation of Israel into the Promised Land. Joshua must have had some trepidation at first, though, for the Lord commanded him not to fear. The Lord said to Joshua,

> "Have I not commanded you? *Be strong and of good courage; do not be afraid*, nor be dismayed, for the Lord your God is with you wherever you go."
> —JOSHUA 1:9

Note that God was not telling Joshua to be like Moses. Rather, God was saying that He would be to Joshua the same source of strength and victory that He had been to Moses.

The Book of Joshua relates how this warrior overcame giants, hostile natives and numerous other challenges, fulfilling his commission courageously.

Fear in the Night

According to Psalm 91 verse 5, we are protected not only from attacks both night and day, but delivered from the *fear* of those attacks.

At night thoughts like these seem to intensify: "What if I lose my job? What if I get sick? What if my marriage fails? What if my children get into trouble?" We may worry about growing old and becoming helpless, about finances or relationships. Seldom mentioned, but not unusual, is the fear that you might lose your mind, as well as the fear of death (see Chapter 11).

"What if…" is one of the greatest fear activators.

Night can be a time when real problems seem more challenging. There is the connotation of a long dark night of the soul, or times of trials that we sometimes go through. We don't escape life's problems (see Chapter 23), but we can be free of the fear that so often accompanies them. Jesus said that in this world we would have tribulation. But He also exhorted, "Be of good cheer, I have overcome the world" (see John 16:33b).

The military has developed night vision goggles that enable soldiers to see objects more clearly and realistically in the dark. In the same way, we can develop "night sight" as God helps us to achieve a different way of looking at dark times, knowing that He is more than able to uphold us.

Anxiety Attacks

> For God did not give us a spirit of timidity (of cowardice, of craven and cringing and fawning fear), but [He has given us a spirit] of power and of love and of calm and well balanced mind and discipline and self control.
> —2 TIMOTHY 1:7 AMP

The above Scripture indicates that an actual evil spirit causes fear. Anxiety attacks, insomnia and nightmares are some manifestations of this spirit.

As born again believers, God assures us that we have authority over evil spirits and *can command the spirit of fear to leave us* (see Psalm 91:13 and Luke 10:19). We must do what Jesus did and quote God's word when the devil harasses us. Jesus told Satan, "It is written...," and then quoted the appropriate verse (see Luke 4:4,8,12).

If these fears plague you, as they did me at one time, it helps to have a written list of Scriptures handy that contain God's promises concerning fear. (You will find just such a list in the appendix.)

I recall putting verses on individual colored note cards and placing them in my wallet, on the refrigerator, on mirrors and even in my car. As I memorized the appropriate verses and repeated them aloud when anxiety arose, the panic attacks became weaker, shorter in duration and less frequent, until they completely disappeared.

That victory over fear was tested a few years ago when our daughter was stationed at an Air Force base in Florida.

A severe hurricane was headed for her area, and she called to tell us that she was leaving immediately to stay with a friend who lived on higher ground: twenty feet above sea level.

"You probably won't hear from me for a while," she said, "but don't worry—God will take care of me."

We prayed together briefly, and I turned her over to the One who loves her even more than I do.

We saw televised reports about the storm's destruction, including a tornado that had touched down in the town she had driven to. The report said that "an unidentified woman was killed." All those Scriptures I memorized came quickly to mind, calming and reassuring me.

Hours later we called the home where she had planned to stay, not really expecting to get through. Her cheery voice answered, assuring us that she was fine. It had taken six hours for her to drive twenty miles because everyone was attempting to flee the storm. Yet she had arrived safely.

"By the way, Mom," she said, "how did you get through? We've tried to call, but all the phone lines are down." Ours was the only call they were able to receive!

We believe we received special help from "heaven's messenger service" to make sure we could hear the good news.

"Don't let the devil rob you of the destiny God has for you. Step out and face your fears. Go ahead and shake, tremble and sweat. God didn't say not to feel fear—He said not to run."

—Joyce Meyer

Chapter 10

The Arrow That Flies by Day

[You shall not fear] the arrow (the evil plots and slanders of the wicked) that flies by day.
–*Psalm 91:5b* AMP

Arrow: symbolically refers to calamity, pain, or sorrow, as well as slander

Many of us have had arrows of slander, gossip or hurtful words hurled at us by misguided people. Pastor David Wilkerson taught on the snare of the fowler in one of his monthly newsletters.[1] He quoted Psalm 119:110: "The wicked have laid a snare for me, yet I erred not from Thy precepts." He said that evil people may resent us because of jealousy, our commitment to Christ or our stand against unrighteousness.

Besides physical harm, the snare could include trying to destroy our peace with emotional abuse.

The devil can also use spiritually blind fellow believers to talk against us, gossip, and try to destroy our reputation. With God's help we will not be trapped by these devices, nor will we give in to bitterness, resentment or revenge. Turn those people over to the Lord and let Him deal with them.

> Do not repay anyone evil for evil. Be careful to do what is right in the eyes of everybody. ...Do not take revenge, my friends, but leave room for God's wrath, for it is written, "It is mine to avenge; I will repay, says the Lord."
> –ROMANS 12:17,19 NIV

Arrows of calamity can fly at us as well. In these times of random violence it's easy to fear even walking down the street in some places. Drive-by shootings, road rage and terrorism all contribute to our sense of being unsafe. Yet God promises protection as we abide in Him. The following story blessed us as it was told to our prayer group.

My prayer partner, Joyce, was returning home from work in downtown Pittsburgh one afternoon. As she walked down the street to her house, she noticed a group of angry young men coming toward her. She heard another group behind her, and it was apparent there would soon be a confrontation between the two gangs. She was trapped between them and quickly asked for God's help.

Joyce heard His voice very strongly in her spirit: "Cross the street *now* and lay down flat on the sidewalk." She had been walking with the Lord for years and was in the habit of obeying Him instantly.

As she lay on the sidewalk, a gang fight erupted, and bullets began flying over her head. Yet Joyce felt such peace. She said it seemed as if there was a warm blanket of protection covering her, a shield that no evil could penetrate.

After the fighting stopped and the groups dispersed, she arose and hurried home. Later the police came to inquire about her well being.

"The neighbors thought you were shot when they saw you lying on the sidewalk. We found bullets in the wall right above where you were lying."

Joyce knows very well Who her shield was that day!

> If God be for us, who [can be] against us? Who can be our foe, if God is on our side?
> —ROMANS 8:31b AMP

As we speak of enemies in our midst, let's briefly revisit Psalm 23. A fresh insight into that well known chapter reveals its application here. Although often read at funerals, it should be considered a psalm for living.

> Though I walk through the [deep, sunless] valley of the shadow of death, I will fear or dread no evil, for You are with me; Your rod [to protect] and Your staff [to guide], they comfort me. You prepare a table before me in the presence of my enemies.
> —PSALM 23:4–5 AMP

Note that God prepares a table (a feast or banquet) in the *presence* of our enemies. Right while we are in the middle of a bad situation, God steps in to "feed" us whatever we need at that moment. He may not immediately pull us out of the situation, but equips us with whatever we need to walk through that valley. Whether our enemies attack us with slander and gossip, or try to physically harm us, God promises protection and guidance.

> No weapon that is formed against you shall prosper, and every tongue that shall rise against you in judgment you shall show to be wrong. This [peace, righteousness, security, triumph over opposition] is the heritage of the servants of the Lord...
> —*ISAIAH 54:17* AMP

Endnotes:

1. David Wilkerson, Times Square Pulpit Series, World Challenge, Lindale, Texas, December 11, 1995.

Psalm 121 NIV

I will lift up my eyes to the hills—
Where does my help come from?
My help comes from the Lord,
The Maker of heaven and earth.

He will not let your foot slip—
He who watches over you will not slumber;
Indeed, He who watches over Israel
Will neither slumber nor sleep.

The Lord watches over you—
The Lord is your shade at your right hand;
The sun will not harm you by day.
Nor the moon by night.

The Lord will keep you from all harm—
He will watch over your life;
The Lord will watch over your coming and going
Both now and forever more.

Chapter 11

Victory Over Death

[You shall not be afraid of] the pestilence that stalks in darkness, nor of the destruction and sudden death that surprise and lay waste at noonday.
—*Psalm 91:6 AMP*

Pestilence: deadly disease; a pernicious or evil agent

It was growing dark as Beth hurried home in a poor neighborhood. She saw a man loitering near a building ahead of her but had no choice except to walk past him. Fear came over her as she approached him, since there had been several muggings in the neighborhood. She sensed an evil presence about the stranger.

Beth whispered a prayer for God's help. She tried to appear confident as she strode past him. He did not, however, make a move toward her. Terror gripped her as she ran into her apartment and locked the door.

Before long she heard sirens and saw police cars approaching the area. A neighbor later told her that someone had been raped at the very spot where she passed that man—only a short while after she got home.

When she phoned the police to offer what information she had, they said a suspect was already in custody. The officers asked if she would come to a police line-up and see if the man she had seen was among the group. She identified the man as the one she had passed on the street, yet wondered why he hadn't attacked her. She was just as vulnerable as the actual victim.

Upon questioning by police, the criminal said he remembered Beth, but didn't attack her because she had "two big guys with her, one on each side"!

Beth knew there were no humans with her, but believed that God had sent angels to accompany her safely home.

No Fear of Death

An often overlooked part of Psalm 91:6 is that we are set free from *fear* of sudden death or calamity.

Fear of death short-circuits many of the adventures and victories we can experience in life. If we have given our hearts to Christ, we know that death is not the end for us, but simply a transition into the next life. It is something we have not experienced, but the outcome is not unknown. God promises it will be a life of joy and peace. Jesus died to take away the sting of death:

> ...that through death He [Jesus] might destroy him who had the power of death, that is, the devil, and release those who through fear of death were all their lifetime subject to bondage.
>
> *–HEBREWS 2:14–15*

Near-death experiences are controversial, and their truthfulness must be considered carefully. Dr. Richard Eby is a credible witness, a Christian physician with a sterling reputation. He wrote about his life-after-life experience in his book, *Caught Up Into Paradise*.[1]

After he fell from a ladder and suffered a serious head injury, Eby's spirit left his body, and he was immediately in Paradise. He became aware that he had a new body; he looked like himself, but was free of pain and fleshly limitations. Being a physician, he describes the new body in detail as having excellent health and perfect vision.

Eby gives us a glimpse of eternal life in Paradise, first noting the indescribable peace, the sense of God's presence, perfect flowers, heavenly music, and a beautiful fragrance that permeates everything. He tells how his mind was incredibly sharp, that he only had to think a question and it was immediately answered.

Others have reported similar stories, especially that experiencing God's love was beyond anything ever felt or even imagined on earth.

> For our earthly bodies, the ones we have now that can die, must be transformed into heavenly bodies that cannot perish but will live forever. When this happens, then at last this Scripture will come true—"Death is swallowed up in victory." O death, where then your victory? Where then your sting?
> –*1 Corinthians 15:53–55 TLB*

It is important to note that we need not rely on earthly witnesses, intriguing as their stories may be. We have the word of God as confirmation.

Heaven, Our Home

When we who are believers pass over to the next life, heaven is our destination. Chapter 21 of the Book of Revelation describes the glory of heaven.

> "And God will wipe away every tear from their eyes; there shall be no more death, nor sorrow, nor crying. There shall be no more pain, for the former things have passed away." Then He who sat on the throne said, "Behold, I make all things new."
> —REVELATION 21:4–5

Read the rest of the chapter and rejoice!

> Eye has not seen, nor ear heard, nor have entered into the heart of man the things that God has prepared for those who love Him.
> —1 CORINTHIANS 2:9

Our Mission

As glorious as heaven our eternal home is, we have been put here on earth for a purpose. We have been given an assignment; we have a divinely appointed destiny. When we are in the secret place, in communion with God, He will reveal the work He has for us.

Often our mission is like an unfolding scroll, with things being revealed little by little. There are times and seasons and places that change as we journey through life.

Scripture says we are not of the world, but we are in the world, and we are called to have a positive effect in our sphere of influence. Those who are older or who have had a brush with death can tell us how brief life is. Whatever stage we are in, we are to make the most of the time and seize every opportunity!

> Teach us to number our days, that we may gain a heart of wisdom.
> —PSALM 90:12

Death of Our Dreams

We can experience a kind of emotional death as we see our dreams slip by. Dreams for a career, a family, relationships, ministry, ours and our children's bright future—even good health or financial security. God is a God of restoration and wants to minister His love, peace and victory. He promises to restore "the years the locusts have eaten" (see Joel 2:25–27).

He reestablished King David after he repented of sin with Bathsheba. Jesus' very own disciple Peter, who had worked closely with Him, denied Christ. Yet after repenting, Peter went on to become a mighty man of God. Caleb was eighty-five years old when he claimed the inheritance God had promised so many years before. (See Joshua 14:11–13.)

As a famous baseball manager once said, "It ain't over till it's over." As long as we are alive, the God of miracles can renew, heal, replenish and restore what the devil has stolen from us. (See Zechariah 9:12b.)

God promises that we will be set free from the fear of sudden death, pestilence and destruction. He promises that we will be healed of mourning over the past and fear of the future. We can walk in confidence and courage and live life to the fullest because He holds us in the palm of His hand.

Never give up or lose hope! Don't be afraid of tomorrow—God is already there.

> For I know the thoughts and plans I have for you, says the Lord, thoughts and plans for welfare and peace and not for evil, to give you hope in your final outcome.
> —*JEREMIAH 29:11* AMP

Endnotes:

1 Richard Eby, *Caught Up Into Paradise*, Fleming H. Revell Co., Old Tappan, NJ, 1971.

Lincoln's Road to the White House

Failed in business in 1831
Defeated for legislature in 1832
Second failure in business in 1833
Suffered a nervous breakdown in 1836
Defeated for Speaker in 1838
Defeated for Elector in 1840
Defeated for Congress in 1848
Defeated for Senate in 1855
Defeated for Vice President in 1856
Defeated for Senate in 1858
Elected President in 1860

Let us not lose heart and grow weary and faint in acting nobly and doing right, for in due time and at the proper season we shall reap, if we do not loosen and relax our courage and faint.

—*Galatians 6:9* AMP

Chapter 12

When Everyone Around You Falls

A thousand may fall at your side, and ten thousand at your right hand; but it shall not come near you.
–*PSALM 91:7*

Fall: to stumble through weakness, to perish, to fall in war, to sink in despondency, to bow down, to bow to an idol, to fall in comparison to another (be inferior), to yield to, to be in great commotion

Some scholars believe that verse 7 refers literally to the Jews crossing the Red Sea, as told in Exodus 14 (see Chapter 13). Or it could concern the story of the plagues in Egypt.

The Jews became slaves in Egypt and cried out to God to deliver them. God sent Moses to Pharaoh demanding that he "let my people go." Exodus chapters 7–11 tell how, when Pharaoh refused to let the Jews leave Egypt, the Lord sent a series of plagues upon the Egyptians. These included bloodied waters, frogs, gnats, flies, boils, hail, locusts, darkness, and finally, death of all the firstborn children and animals.

Although the Jews lived right in the middle of all this, none of the plagues touched them! God sovereignly put a hedge of protection around them, even in the midst of devastation. He will do the same for us.

In my own family, God has shown His Divine protection in the midst of calamity. My nieces Mary Beth and JoAnn were young career women, happy to be living in the appealing climate of southern Florida. Having formerly lived in New Jersey, they basked in the year-round warmth of the Miami area. Yet tragedy came upon that place during Hurricane Andrew, a devastating storm that caused mass destruction.

The storm was not supposed to hit their area, but when it took a sudden turn, people tried to flee from its path. Roads were jammed, and the girls had no way of escape. They were forced to stay in their apartment, right in the path of the hurricane.

Mary Beth and JoAnn barricaded themselves in the bathroom, a small space in the middle of their home, and prayed for God's deliverance. They heard fierce wind, loud crashes, sirens and the sound of heavy rains all around them. The storm seemed to last for hours, but the walls around them stood.

When things finally quieted down they left the bathroom and were appalled at what they saw. The outer walls of their building had collapsed, the shopping center across the street was all but gone, and there was total destruction everywhere. Yet in that tiny bathroom they were safe. They thanked God for preserving them.

He [God] is a shield to those who trust and take refuge in Him.
—PROVERBS 30:5 AMP

What else does *fall* mean? Other definitions include these:

Stumbling through weakness was discussed at length in Chapter 6. Here is a Biblical promise that God will help us when we do stumble:

The steps of a good man are ordered by the Lord, and He delights in his way. Though he fall, he shall not be utterly cast down; for the Lord upholds him with His hand.
—PSALM 37:23–24

To sink in despondency: Depression and despair are rampant in our society today. With so many bad things happening, it is easy to be affected. Sometimes grief can overwhelm us. The Lord can heal these sorrows:

[God has sent Jesus] to grant [consolation and joy] to those who mourn in Zion—to give them an ornament (a garland or diadem) of beauty instead of ashes, the oil of joy instead of mourning, the garment [expressive] of praise instead of a heavy, burdened, and failing spirit—that they might be called oaks of righteousness [lofty, strong, and magnificent, distinguished for uprightness, justice and right standing with God], the planting of the Lord, that He may be glorified.
—ISAIAH 61:3 AMP

Idolatry has many meanings, but it is basically giving preference to something other than the one true God. Idols can include possessions, a job, social status, friends, even being in awe of and deferring to rich and powerful people. We have a choice in what we worship, for the Lord commands:

> Little children, keep yourselves from idols (false gods)—[from anything and everything that would occupy the place in your heart due to God, from any sort of substitute for Him that would take first place in your life].
> —*1 John 5:21 AMP*

To feel inferior: Poor self image has many causes, but God can heal this and keep you from being ensnared again. You are made in His image, beautiful in His sight.

> You formed my inward parts; You covered me in my mother's womb. I will praise You, for I am fearfully and wonderfully made. ... My frame was not hidden from You, when I was made in secret... Your eyes saw my substance, being yet unformed... How also precious are Your thoughts to me, O God! How great is the sum of them! If I should count them, they would be more in number than the sand.
> —*Psalm 139:13–17*

To be in great commotion: Many of us lead hectic, noisy, crowded lives, and chaos might easily overwhelm us. The Lord will be our refuge in such times. God's peace is said to pass all understanding, meaning that it is beyond human ability to create or comprehend.

> Peace I leave with you; My [own] peace I now give and bequeath to you. Not as the world gives do I give to you. Do not let your heart be troubled, neither let them be afraid. [Stop allowing yourselves to be agitated and

disturbed; and do not permit yourselves to be fearful and intimidated and cowardly and unsettled].
—*JOHN 14:27 AMP*

The Lord's amazing protection over those who boldly trust Him to keep them from falling into destruction is illustrated by this story of John G. Lake. It demonstrates that God's power to protect is greater than the power of evil.

John G. Lake had a preaching and healing ministry from 1898 to 1935. During that time thousands were miraculously healed by the Lord's power flowing through Lake.

One time Lake was ministering to people who had bubonic plague. When asked if he was afraid of contracting the disease, Lake affirmed that the Spirit of the Living God working through him was greater than any disease. At one point, he placed the contaminated saliva of a victim on his own hand, and when skeptics looked at it through a microscope, the germs died right before their eyes!

As for God, His way is perfect! The Word of the Lord is tested and tried; He is a shield to all those who take refuge and put their trust in Him.
—*PSALM 18:30 AMP*

Chapter 13

Your Place of Safety

> Only a spectator shall you be [yourself inaccessible in the secret place of the Most High] as you witness the reward of the wicked.
> —PSALM 91:8 AMP

Inaccessible: unapproachable, not able to be reached

The enemy was in hot pursuit and well equipped for battle. Defeat seemed inevitable to the weary band of Israelites fleeing for their lives.

Pharaoh had ordered his army to pursue the slaves who had recently left Egypt. The Israelites were trapped between the advancing army and the Red Sea (see Exodus 14). There seemed to be no way of escape until God parted the waters of the Red Sea, allowing His people to cross safely to the other side.

The Egyptian army was close behind them, with horses, chariots, and well armed troops. They followed the Israelites across the divine roadway, but when the last Jew was safely across the sea and multitudes of the enemy were on the pathway, the waters of the Red Sea were no longer held back. Walls of water crashed down on Pharaoh's army as God's people watched in amazement. From their place of safety they witnessed the army of the nation that had enslaved and abused them for hundreds of years be swept away by raging waters.

God is more than able to deal with our enemies as we yield to Him. Yet it is important to note that He is the one who will take revenge, not us. A famous politician was heard to say, "Don't get mad—get even." God says, "Vengeance is Mine, I will repay" (see Deuteronomy 32:35). This is discussed further in Chapter 10.

There are times when we are to fight, as in a combat situation, or when our lives are threatened. Yet God will often step in and take care of evil people who persecute, harass or threaten us. It's interesting to hear of the various ways He has done so.

We already made reference to the book of Esther, chapter 7, where we read how righteous Mordecai saw his persecutor, Haman, hung on the very gallows Haman had prepared for Mordecai. In Chapter 14 we'll read how God threw the enemies of Jehoshaphat and the Jews into confusion and gave Judah a great victory (see 2 Chronicles 20). In another dramatic rescue, God sent an angel to kill the entire army of the Assyrian king as he prepared to attack King Hezekiah and the Jews (see 2 Chronicles 32:21–22).

Here is a contemporary story of experiencing God's power to rescue while only observing the danger and not having to fight. It was told to me by a prayer partner in Baltimore, Maryland.

My friend Phyllis and several other elderly women were on their way home from a Christian seminar in Washington, DC, when their car broke down. It was after midnight when they got lost in what she described as "a bad neighborhood" where the surroundings looked quite threatening. A group of young men stood on one street corner, and another gang stood on the opposite side.

Each group started toward the car. The women prayed aloud for God's help, then began to sing worship songs. Suddenly, out of nowhere, a motorcycle policeman appeared and was soon joined by two others. The young men retreated, as the officers quickly worked on the car and got it running again.

The only words the policemen spoke to the driver were directions to the main highway, with an admonition not to stop until they left the city.

As quickly as they had arrived, the motorcyclists disappeared—without making a sound! Phyllis and her friends knew that it was Divine intervention that had saved them that night.

> He will guard the feet of his saints, but the wicked shall be silent in darkness.
> —*1 Samuel 2:9*

> You are my hiding place; You shall preserve me from trouble; You shall surround me with songs of deliverance.
> —*Psalm 32:7*

This is a psalm of David, a song of thanksgiving and victory written when the Lord had delivered him from his many enemies, including King Saul.

Psalm 18

Lord, how I love You!
For you have done such tremendous things for me.
The Lord is my fort where I can enter and be safe;
No one can follow me in and slay me.
He is a rugged mountain where I hide;
He is my Savior, a rock where none can reach me,
And a tower of safety.
He is my shield.
He is like the strong horn of a mighty fighting bull.
All I need to do is cry to Him—oh, praise the Lord
And I am saved from all my enemies!

–Psalm 18:1–3 TLB

Chapter 14

No Evil Shall Befall You

> Because you have made the Lord your refuge, and the Most High your dwelling place, there shall no evil befall you, nor any plague or calamity come near your tent.
> —*Psalm 91:9–10* AMP

Calamity: a grave misfortune, great distress, troublesome evil, sad event or accident

The leader faced an impossible situation. His country was threatened with attack by a vast army of warriors from several surrounding nations. His army was greatly outnumbered, and things seemed hopeless. King Jehoshaphat and his countrymen knew they had only one recourse if they were to survive: They fasted and prayed for God's protection.

The Lord's prophet then said to them,

> "Do not be afraid nor dismayed because of this great multitude, for *the battle is not yours, but God's*.... You will not need to fight in this battle. Position yourselves, stand still and see the salvation of the Lord, who is with

you, O Judah and Jerusalem! Do not fear or be dismayed; tomorrow go out against them, for the Lord is with you."
–2 CHRONICLES 20:15–17

Early in the morning the king and his troops set out for the desert of Tekoa. The praisers went first, singing songs to the Lord. As they went forth, before they even reached the battle site, the enemies of Judah were thrown into confusion and began to attack each other. Jehoshaphat and his men did not have to fight at all, yet their enemies were completely defeated.

When the Jews came to a place that overlooked the battle area, they saw only dead bodies of enemy soldiers lying on the ground. No one had escaped. There was so much plunder that it took three days for Jehoshaphat and his army to collect it all. They returned joyfully to Jerusalem and went to the temple to praise the Lord.

Another interesting effect of this event was that the fear of God came upon Judah's enemies. When they saw how God fought for His people, they left Judah alone for many years. The kingdom of Jehoshaphat enjoyed a long period of peace and rest (see 2 Chronicles 20:1–30).

The word *tent* in verse 10 can also refer to our homes or households, where God extends His protection. This is illustrated in a story told by Corrie Ten Boom in her book, *Marching Orders for the End Battle*.[1]

The Ten Boom family provided hiding places for persecuted Jews in Holland during World War II. When the family was caught, Corrie spent time in Nazi concentration camps, but never lost her faith. After her release from prison, Corrie traveled all over the world telling her story, ministering hope and encouragement.

During one visit to the Congo, Corrie observed that Christians there were under terrible persecution. In one village, a group of rebels advanced on a school where 200 children of missionaries lived. The rebels planned to kill both the children and their teachers.

Knowing of the danger, people at the school began to pray. Their only physical protection was a fence plus a few soldiers, while the enemy had several hundred troops. Just as the insurgents approached the dwelling, they suddenly stopped, turned around and ran away.

This happened the next day, and again on the third day. One of the wounded rebels was brought to the mission hospital, and the doctor asked why his army had not attacked the school as they had planned.

The man replied, "We could not do it because we saw hundreds of soldiers in white uniforms and we became scared."

In Africa at that time and place, soldiers never wore white uniforms, so the Christians concluded that they must have seen angels.

> The angel of the Lord encamps around those who fear Him [—who revere and worship Him with awe] and each of them He delivers.
> *—Psalm 34:7 AMP*

There have been other reports where the Lord opened the eyes of the enemy to see multitudes of angels protecting His people. We who are God's children need not see them, but need only to be thankful for their protection.

So he [Elisha] answered, "Do not fear [the large invading army], for those who are with us are more than those who are with them."

And Elisha prayed, and said, "Lord, I pray, open his eyes that he may see." Then the Lord opened the eyes of the young man, and he saw. And behold the mountain was full of horses and chariots of fire all around Elisha.

−2 KINGS 6:16–17

Endnotes:

1 Corrie Ten Boom, *Marching Orders for the End Battle*, Christian Literature Crusade, Fort Washington, PA.

Psalm 37

Do not fret because of evildoers,
Nor be envious of the workers of iniquity.
For they shall soon be cut down like grass,
And wither as the green herb.

Trust in the Lord and do good;
Dwell in the land, and feed on His faithfulness.
Delight yourself also in the Lord,
And He shall give you the desires of your heart.

Commit your way to the Lord,
Trust also in Him, and He shall bring it to pass.
He shall bring forth your righteousness as the light,
And your justice as the noonday.

Rest in the Lord, and wait patiently for Him;
Do not fret because of him who prospers in his way...
For evil doers shall be cut off;
But those who wait on the Lord,
They shall inherit the earth...

But the salvation of the righteous is from the Lord;
He is their strength in the time of trouble.
And the Lord shall help them and deliver them;
He shall deliver them from the wicked,
And save them,
Because they trust in Him.

–Psalm 37: 1–9, 39–40

Chapter 15

Angels Will Guard You

> For He will give His angels [especial] charge over you, to accompany and defend and preserve you in all your ways [of obedience and service].
> —*Psalm 91:11* AMP

Angel: sent one, messenger

Much has been written about angels and how they apparently come to the aid of those in need. Yet it is important to acknowledge that it is God, not angels, who rescues.

We are told clearly in Scripture that these spirit beings are not to be worshipped. The Book of Revelation reveals this truth during an exchange between the Apostle John and an angelic messenger:

> And I fell at his [the angel's] feet to worship him. But he said to me, "See that you do not do that! I am your fellow servant, and of your brethren who have the testimony of Jesus. Worship God!"
> —*Revelation 19:10*

The first chapter of the Book of Hebrews tells us that angels worship God (verse 6), are messengers (verse 7), and are sent to help and care for those people who will receive salvation (verse 14).

We are not to seek angelic experiences or visitations. There is the danger that we can conjure up the wrong spirit. Evil spirit beings can appear as good angels, out to deceive and harm us. Scripture cautions that the devil can appear as "an angel of light" (see 2 Corinthians 11:14). God will send angels to help us if and when we need them. Often they appear in human form, or may not be seen at all. We might only be aware of their action to rescue us, without seeing any physical presence.

As a teenager I experienced rescue from certain death, and know now that it was Divine intervention. Here is what happened that day in the Atlantic Ocean.

Dark waters engulfed me as I went under for the third time, pulled by a strong undertow. Fear had not set in because, after all, I was only fourteen years old. I felt invincible and expected to live forever. I swam in this ocean every day all summer and never had a problem.

But that day I foolishly swam near a jetty in an area where there were no lifeguards. As I came to the surface I saw there was no one else in the water, nor on the nearest beach area. Exhausted from struggling against the undertow, I finally realized I didn't have the strength to fight the current and I was in trouble.

I sputtered, "God, I could use some help."

The words were scarcely out of my mouth when I heard a voice behind me asking, "Do you need help?"

"Yes," I gulped.

When I turned and saw that the voice belonged to an old baldheaded man, my hope dwindled. I was much younger and stronger than he—how could he rescue me? But when he grabbed my hand and pulled me toward the shore, I was amazed at his incredible strength.

As we neared the beach he asked, "Can you make it from here?"

"Yes, thanks!"

He didn't say another word.

I climbed onto the beach and put my head down to catch my breath. When I looked up a moment later to thank my rescuer, he was gone! I don't know where he came from, nor who he was, but God sent help and saved my life.

> Call to Me and I will answer you and show you great and mighty things... which you do not know (do not distinguish and recognize, have knowledge of and understand).
> —*Jeremiah 33:3 AMP*

Recently we heard a story about a three-year-old boy who had been crushed beneath a heavy automatic garage door. When his mother found him, she believed he was dead, but CPR brought the child back to life. Little Brian was severely injured and not expected to survive. If he did, brain damage seemed inevitable. Miraculously, Brian recovered in a few days and was sent home.

About a month later, when the child woke from his afternoon nap, he told his mother this amazing story. He usually spoke in small phrases, but used whole sentences when he related this episode.

He said that when he was stuck under the garage door, the pain was bad. When he called out to his mother, she could not hear him.

"And then the birdies came," he said.

Upon questioning, he replied that they made a whooshing sound and were beautiful, dressed in white. They told him "the baby" (his lifeless body on the garage floor that he apparently looked down upon) would be all right.

Brian also related exactly what his mother had said when she found him apparently dead. He accurately described his treatment by paramedics and the trip in the ambulance.

Brian's mother realized her little one's "birdies" were probably angels, but *angel* was not in his vocabulary.

The child said he and "the birdies" flew through the air very fast, and went on a trip far away. He saw a beautiful warm bright light that was very comforting to him. Someone in the light put His arms around the child and told him how much He loved him, but that he had to go back to Earth. Then the Person in the light kissed him good-bye. Brian and the angels flew through the clouds, back to his hospital room.

The story went on for an hour. Brian said the birdies are always with us, but we can't see them, except with our hearts. He said that we all have a plan that we must live out, and that "the birdies help us to do that because they love us so much."

> Are not the angels all ministering spirits (servants) sent out in the service [of God for the assistance] of those who are to inherit salvation?
> *–HEBREWS 1:14* AMP

Chapter 16

Heavenly Helpers

> They [angels] will lift you up in their hands, so that you will not strike your foot against a stone.
> *—Psalm 91:12 NIV*

Lift up: to be held high, to carry from a lower to a higher position, to raise in value

He chose to obey God and went into the desert to fast for forty days. Afterward, Jesus was hungry and weary. It was at this point that the devil came to tempt Him, as he often does us.

In Matthew 4:5–11 we read how the devil quoted Psalm 91:12 to entice Jesus to prove His divinity. He challenged Christ, "If you are the Son of God, throw Yourself down [from here, the pinnacle of the temple]. For it is written: 'He shall give His angels charge over you to keep you,' and 'In their hands they shall bear you up, lest you dash your foot against a stone'" (AMP).

Jesus did not yield to this temptation to flaunt His power. Note how the devil tried to get Jesus to doubt by saying, "*If* you are the Son of God…" Yet, in that desert place, He stood firm against the devil's taunts as an example for us.

As a human, Jesus was fully able to experience physical discomfort as well as temptation. It is encouraging to note that even He received Divine assistance in time of need. Verse 11 tells us that "the devil left Him, and behold, angels came and ministered to Him."

How often have we been harassed when we were at a low point—physically, mentally or spiritually—tempted to take an easy way out? The devil has challenged our faith by saying, in effect, "If God really loved you...," or "If you trust God why don't you...," or "Did God really say...?"

Doubt-generating mind games are prime weapons the devil uses to get us off track. In such times we need to do what Christ did: quote God's word. When Satan tried to tempt Him, Jesus replied, "It is written...."

If we are to reply likewise, we need to know what "is written" in the Bible and use God's word as an offensive and defensive weapon in the battle against the devil. That's a good reason to study and memorize Scripture.

In the book *Angels Among Us*[1] Deborah Jacobson tells how angels literally bore her daughter Traci up so she would not be dashed against the rocks.

Traci went on a senior class camping trip in the remote Cascade Mountains where the elevation was about 3,200 feet. Back at home, Traci's mother woke that night with a strong leading to pray fervently for her daughter's safety. After a while peace came over Deborah, a confidence that God was protecting Traci. She drifted off to sleep.

A late night phone call brought news that Traci had been injured in a fall. When the teen was safely back home, she told her parents this amazing story.

Traci and friends were riding bikes along a winding mountain trail as darkness fell. She had an accident and was thrown from her bike—over the cliff.

She hit some rocks on the way down and bounced into the air. There was nothing to stop her from falling thousands of feet down the mountain. It was pitch dark by this time, and she could see nothing. When she bounced off the first ledge, she said "someone" caught her in mid-air.

"I don't know who, Mom," Traci said. "I couldn't *see* anyone, but I *felt* them. I know it sounds weird, but someone caught me in the air... held me in their arms for a while, then gently laid me down on the rocks just like they were laying me down on my bed."

Amazingly, Traci had only minor injuries. The family knows that God responded to a mother's prayer and sent help to "bear Traci up" lest she be dashed against the rocks.

There is a difference between claiming God's promise of safety and acting with foolishness or presumption. Daredevils are not guaranteed Divine protection. Risk-takers who violate the laws of nature and common sense for personal thrills do so at their own peril. Yet there are times to take great risks, such as to save a life, take a stand for righteousness or obey the Lord's clear direction.

Mel Tari[2] was part of an evangelical team in Indonesia who saw the Lord perform many miracles in their behalf. These wonders were necessary for them to survive and preach the Gospel.

During the rainy season there, it can rain for as long as forty days, making travel difficult. On one occasion the group was in Timor where they had to cross the Noemina River. There was no bridge, so they had to ford the river on foot. The water is about 300 yards wide and over twenty feet deep at flood stage.

Local natives cautioned the evangelists not to try to cross the river, because they would surely drown in its swift current. However, the ministers felt strongly that the Lord had told them to cross right then and not wait.

Believing He would take care of them as they obeyed, the leader set foot into the river. With that first step water came to his ankles, and the same with the next steps. The stream never came higher than his knees. The team followed him and crossed safely.

They said they kept thinking of the Scripture verse in Isaiah 43:2 that says, "When you pass through the waters, I will be with you; and when you pass through the rivers, they will not sweep over you" (NIV).

The natives were astonished because they knew the water was twenty or thirty feet deep. After the team was safely on the other side, onlookers attempted to cross and nearly drowned in the deep and swiftly moving river.

You'll recall a similar story in Exodus 14. It describes how God parted the Red Sea to allow Moses and the Jewish people to cross. When Pharaoh's army pursued them, God no longer held back the water, so the enemy troops perished.

God is able to do whatever is necessary to protect His people. He will supply anything required when He gives us a task. If we operate under His clear direction, then lack of education, finances, health or other adverse circumstances will not hinder His work from flowing through us.

God has a plan for your life, so go for it! Boldly pursue the course set before you and watch God perform wonders in your behalf.

> I am the Lord, the God of all mankind. Is anything too hard for me?
> —*JEREMIAH 32:27 NIV*

Endnotes:

1. Joan Wester Anderson, *Angels Among Us*, Guideposts Associates, Inc., Carmel, NY 10512, 1992.
2. Mel Tari and Cliff Dudley, *Like A Mighty Wind*, Creation House, Carol Stream, IL, 1971.

Chapter 17

Power Over Lions and Snakes

You shall tread upon the lion and the cobra; the young lion and the serpent shall you trample under foot.
–PSALM 91:13

Tread: to trample, march on, crush under foot

A well known traveler sat by the campfire enjoying the company of the island folk. As he reached into the brush pile for more fuel for the fire, a deadly snake struck his hand and held on. Onlookers expected him to swell up immediately and then fall dead, as had happened to other victims in the past. After watching for a while and observing no ill effects, they concluded that the Apostle Paul must have been a god.

This story is recounted in the Book of Acts, chapter 28. It verifies the promise Jesus gave to His followers, quoted in Mark 16:18, that believers will not be harmed by snake bites or poisonous substances they accidentally ingest. Many missionaries have relied on this promise as they ate an unknown delicacy prepared for them by indigenous people in a foreign land. (Note that this promise does not apply to those who deliberately test God by handling poisonous snakes or ingesting poison.)

In this portion of Psalm 91, the lion represents a bold, strong creature, either good or evil. In verse 13 it is an evil one that might stalk its prey, capture it, then tear it to pieces. The young lion is aggressive, seeking and seizing his victim. The older lion has less hunting strength, but waits for prey to wander into its territory.

Snakes in Scripture usually allude to demonic influences. A cobra is a snake that coils itself and waits for the opportune moment to strike its victim. It represents a sneaky attack, whereas a serpent (or dragon) is a fiery reptile that attacks openly and aggressively with blazing fire.

Most of us do not experience literal attacks by lions or snakes, but it is interesting to consider what these creatures might represent in our own lives. The young lion could portray events that happen to us suddenly, without warning: accidents, illness, job loss, or economic calamity. There could also be physical attacks by violent, hostile people, or natural disasters such as tornadoes.

The old lion can symbolize things we know might occur in the future, such as declining income, old age, or changing family situations.

The snake has been called "low down and sneaky," and might characterize subtle problems such as worry, or attacks on the mind such as depression.

One of the more malevolent spirits is a demon assigned to cause one to consider or attempt suicide. Reverend Jack Hayford (Pastor of Church on the Way, Van Nuys, California) believes there are literal demons whose job it is to do exactly that. Things that sneak up on us could also include broken relationships, unexpected expenses, and family problems.

The good news is that God promises His followers power to tread on these enemies. The word *tread* in the original language is a strong term meaning to trample, march on, or crush under foot. Evil might pursue us, but with the help of God Almighty, it need not overwhelm or destroy us.

In the next chapter we will learn about the power of God's name. We'll find that when we fight an enemy "in the name of Jesus Christ," great power is unleashed in our behalf.

The Bible gives examples of men (such as Joshua and King David) whom the Lord instructed to fight, and to whom He promised victory. Other times the person was unable to rescue himself from evil consequences thrust upon him when he obeyed the Lord. He had to rely completely on God's divine intervention, as did Daniel in the lion's den (see Daniel 6:19–27).

Occasionally circumstances may cause us to be too weak physically, mentally or spiritually to fight the onslaught of the devil. At such times God promises His followers that He Himself will step on the serpent in our behalf.

> The God of peace will soon crush Satan under your feet.
> —*Romans 16:20a NIV*

Sometimes calamity awaits us and we have no idea what is about to happen. Even without a battle on our part, God often stops the destruction before it can harm us. The following story, printed in a local newspaper, illustrates such an event.

Jim Jordan is a long distance truck driver who told this story to Bart Lindeman, a reporter for the Greensburg, Pennsylvania, *Tribune-Review*.[1]

One snowy winter night Jordan was driving his rig over an expressway that had occasional slick spots. There were few other vehicles on the road, but when Jordan passed a tanker truck he noticed a flicker of light in the rear of the tanker. When the light disappeared, he thought it might have been his imagination. Yet Jordan slowed, dropping behind the truck to observe. In a few minutes the light appeared again and became constant. The experienced road warrior soon realized that the tanker's right rear trailer brakes were on fire, and the fire was building quickly.

Jordan tried to contact the driver by CB radio, but there was no response for some time. Eventually a faint voice answered, and Jordan told the driver what he observed.

Immediately the tanker slowed and pulled off to the side of the road, with Jordan parking a safe distance behind him. Jordan grabbed a fire extinguisher, jumped out of the cab, and ran to the truck ahead. The driver tried in vain to pack snow around the brake drum.

Jordan pulled the fire extinguisher's safety pin and handed it to the driver. By carefully spraying into the brake drum, the men were able to put out the fire.

After a few minutes, the trucker thanked Jordan, commenting that he had no fire extinguisher in his rig. After a long pause, the driver continued. "If that fire had reached my tanks, this whole area, even that mountain, would have been wiped out. Neither of us would be here."

When Jordan asked what his cargo was, the driver replied: "Rocket fuel."

Before he left, the tanker driver turned and made this final comment: "The good Lord was sitting on my shoulder tonight. I don't know how you reached me and got me stopped. My radio hasn't worked all day."

Whether we are pursued by serpents of loneliness, fear, financial ruin, or lions of physical harm, disasters, or family problems, God promises that we will tread these enemies under foot. As we obey Him, He will give us victory over all the power of the enemy!

> Behold! I have given you authority and power to trample upon serpents and scorpions, and [physical and mental strength and ability] over all the power that the enemy [possesses]; and nothing shall in any way harm you.
> –*LUKE 10:19* AMP

Endnotes:
1 Tribune-Review Publishing Company, Cabin Hill Drive, Greensburg, PA 15601; August 22, 1997, p. A8.

Chapter 18

Just a Coincidence?

> Because he has set his love upon Me, therefore I will deliver him; I will set him on high, because he knows and understands My name [has a personal knowledge of My mercy, love and kindness—trusts and relies on Me, knowing I will never forsake him, no, never].
> —*Psalm 91:14 AMP*

Deliver: from the Hebrew word *palat*, meaning to cause to escape, rescue, carry away

Setting one's love on God and knowing His name are conditions for receiving this promise of deliverance. The word *deliver* (*natsal*) in verse 3 of Psalm 91 has the meaning of being snatched out of a problem. But here in verse 14 the Hebrew word (*palat*) gives the idea that one is allowed to go through a problem for a time, but then will be rescued by the Lord.

Missionaries and men in battle can attest to this kind of liberation, as seen in some of the stories in this book. And, if we think carefully about it, most of us can recall a time of unusual rescue from a bad situation. Perhaps we called it coincidence, a lucky break, or fortuitous timing. Most likely it was God Himself who provided the means of escape for us. Here is an episode in my own life where the Lord intervened with special "roadside assistance."

Little did I know how my faith would be tested and then strengthened that bitterly cold day in Maryland. As I drove carefully down the small private road in our housing subdivision, our old Country Squire station wagon got stuck on a patch of ice. It was only about 200 feet from the main highway, where the road surface appeared dry and clear.

Despite my best efforts, the car would not move. It was too heavy for me push, and there was little hope of help arriving soon. Few people were at home in my small neighborhood during the day.

I was afflicted with Myasthenia Gravis, a neuromuscular disease, and did not have the strength to walk for help or hike the half mile uphill to my house. I began to feel numb in the cold weather. I was also concerned that a vehicle might turn in from the main road, unexpectedly hit the patch of ice, and crash into my vehicle.

It seemed to be a difficult situation with no apparent solution except one—prayer. In recent years, physical weakness had drawn me closer to the Lord and helped me to develop a trust in His care and provision.

I leaned my head on the steering wheel, closed my eyes and asked God to help me. The prayer was scarcely finished when I felt a tap on the back bumper of the car. A glance in the rearview mirror revealed a tow truck! I remember thinking, "Where did he come from?"

I had driven past the few houses on our road earlier and had seen no such vehicle, and the road I was on was the only way in and out of the development. He could not have entered without passing me along the way.

Without a word the tow truck pushed my car off the ice and onto the dry main highway. I pulled over to the shoulder of the road to get out and thank my rescuer. When I looked back, all I saw was a white unmarked tow truck disappearing over the hill.

Try as I might, I was unable to find out who the vehicle belonged to. Towing companies and service station managers all assured me their tow trucks were clearly marked.

I don't know where the rescuer came from, nor where he went, but I know that God took care of me, just as He promised He always would.

> He [God] holds victory in store for the upright, he is a shield to those whose walk is blameless, for he guards the course of the just and protects the way of his faithful ones.
>
> –*PROVERBS 2:7–8 NIV*

Battlefront veterans can often relate experiences of Divine intervention. The following story was in Cindy Jacob's book, *Possessing the Gates of the Enemy*.[1]

In 1940 British Prime Minister Winston Churchill was advised that Nazi war planes were about to launch an invasion. Churchill knew that German factories were able to produce many more planes than Britain at that time, and the Royal Air Force would be greatly outnumbered. The attack began with over 200 Nazi planes, with only 26 fighters launched by the RAF.

Then the German forces turned around and headed back. Without apparent reason, 185 of their planes had gone down in flames, and they were retreating. Miraculously the RAF had won the battle!

Amazing reports came back from captured Nazi pilots. When asked why they turned back when so few were attacking, they exclaimed that hundreds of British planes were in the battle.

"Where did you get all those planes you threw into the battle over Britain?" a Luftwaffe officer asked his British interrogator. Actually there were only a handful of outmoded RAF Spitfire and Hurricane fighters arrayed against the powerful German Air Force.

Later a captured Nazi officer said he knew the British had a secret weapon that was connected to the striking of Big Ben at nine o'clock every night. Unknown to them, that weapon was a moment of silent prayer that went up throughout Britain at that hour. Once again Divine intervention was apparent.

> Do not fear... The Lord your God in your midst, the Mighty one, will save; He will rejoice over you with gladness, He will quiet you with His love, He will rejoice over you with singing.
> *—ZEPHANIAH 3:16–17*

Endnotes:

1. Cindy Jacobs, *Possessing the Gates of the Enemy*, Chosen Books, Fleming H. Revell Co., Tarrytown, NY, 1991, p. 52 (quoting Pollard Carter's book, *Hand on the Helm*).

Psalm 46

God is our refuge and strength
[Mighty and impenetrable to temptation],
A very present and well-proved help in trouble.
Therefore we will not fear, though the earth should change
And though the mountains be shaken into the midst of the seas...

The nations raged, the kingdoms tottered and were moved;
He uttered His voice, the earth melted.
The Lord of hosts is with us; the God of Jacob is our refuge
(Our Fortress and High Tower).

Come, behold the works of the Lord,
Who has wrought desolation and wonders in the earth.
He makes wars to cease to the ends of the earth;
He breaks the bow into pieces and snaps the spear in two;
He burns the chariots in the fire.

Let be and be still, and know (recognize and understand)
That I am God. I will be exalted among the nations!
I will be exalted in the earth!

The Lord of hosts is with us;
The God of Jacob is our Refuge
(Our High Tower and Stronghold).

-From the Amplified Bible

Chapter 19

What's in a Name?

> Because he has set his love upon Me, therefore will I deliver him; I will set him on high, because he knows and understands My name [has a personal knowledge of My mercy, love and kindness—trusts and relies on Me, knowing I will never forsake him, no, never].
> –*PSALM 91:14* AMP

Name: that which distinguishes one person from another; in Scripture, denotes the nature, properties and significance of a person

In biblical times, names had great significance, often making statements about the character, reputation or authority of a person.

For example, the Apostle named Joses (Acts 4:36) was called *Barnabas*, which means "encourager." The Apostles valued Barnabas' compassion and help. *Abraham* means "father of a great multitude." Jesus told *Peter* he was the rock upon which His church would be built.

A name was also considered an extension of the person himself. To speak "in the name of" was to express the thoughts or authority of that person. The name of the

Lord is to be exalted, and that is why God gave the commandment, "Thou shalt not take the name of the Lord in vain," that is, use it disrespectfully (see Exodus 20:7).

We are told to pray "in the name of Jesus" to identify ourselves with Him and His values. We can have complete confidence that He hears and answers, according to this promise:

> And I [Jesus] will do [I Myself will grant] whatever you ask in My name [as presenting all that I AM], so that the Father may be glorified and extolled in (through) the Son. [Yes] I will grant [I Myself will do for you] whatever you shall ask in My Name [as presenting all that I AM].
> –*John 14:13–14* AMP

God is referred to by many different names in Scripture. Each name represents an aspect of His character. *Immanuel*, meaning "God with us," is the Old Testament reference to God as the coming Messiah.

Compound names make extended statements about their bearer. *Jehovah* (from the original *Yahweh*, the covenant name of God) means "Lord God," or "the One who is always present." Thus we see the prefix *Jehovah-* attached to some of the names of God. *El-* is another prefix for "God" and probably comes from a root word that means to be strong.

Here are some of God's names listed in the Bible:

Name	Meaning	Reference
Jehovah-Jireh	God the Provider	Genesis 22:14
Jehovah-Rapha	God the Healer	Exodus 15:26
Jehovah-M'Kaddesh	God the Sanctifier	Leviticus 20:8
Jehovah-Shalom	God of Peace	Judges 6:24
Jehovah-Roi	God the Shepherd	Psalm 23:1
El Shaddai	Almighty God	Genesis 21:33

These references describe Jesus:

Title	Reference
Prince of Peace, Wonderful Counselor, Mighty God	Isaiah 9:6
The Way, The Truth, The Life	John 14:6
Lord God Almighty	Revelation 15:3
The Resurrection and The Life	John 11:25
Alpha and Omega	Revelation 1:8
King of Kings	Revelation 17:14

Well known evangelist Reverend Billy Graham relates a story his wife remembered from the years she grew up in China.[1]

Tigers that lived in the region sometimes attacked and killed people. A young woman was walking with her baby tied to her back and a little child beside her when she heard a roar. Terrified, she looked around to see a mother tigress springing at her, followed by two cubs.

The illiterate woman had never attended school or church, but had heard a missionary say that "Jesus is able to help you when you are in trouble." As the tiger clawed at her arm and shoulder, the woman cried out, "Oh, Jesus, help me!" Suddenly the ferocious beast turned and ran away.

Another story of Divine rescue was told in *Guideposts Magazine*.[2] A construction worker fell into a deep muddy ditch his crew had been digging. Everyone else had gone to lunch, and he was alone on this mountain in Oregon. He was completely immersed in water, and his boots were stuck in mud up to his shins.

As he struggled to escape, he sank deeper. As the mud reached his chest, he cried out, "Oh, God, please help."

He continued to sink until his body was completely submerged under the mud. When he could no longer hold his breath, he blacked out.

The next thing he knew, he was lying face down on the ground next to the ditch, as if someone had lifted him to safety. He looked around, but said, "No one was there—no muddy footprints, no tracks, no evidence of help... except for His."

Call upon God for help, just as these people did. Whether you need God the Healer, God the Provider, the God of Peace, or God the Savior, He will be exactly what you require at that moment.

> The name of the Lord is a strong tower; the righteous run to it and are safe.
> —*PROVERBS 18:10*

Endnotes:
1 Billy Graham, *Angels, God's Secret Agents*.
2 *Guideposts Magazine*, New York, NY, January, 1997, p. 31.

Praying in the Name of Jesus:

*"In My name," that is, "My nature."
Not—"You shall use My name as a magic
wand," but—"You will be so intimate with Me
that you will be one with Me." That is a day of
undisturbed relationship between God and the
saint.*

*By the Holy Spirit we can be lifted into such a
relationship with the Father that we are at one
with the perfect sovereign will of God by our free
choice, even as Jesus was.*

–Oswald Chambers
My Utmost for His Highest

Chapter 20

The Great Escape

He shall call upon Me, and I will answer him.
—PSALM 91:15

Answer: to reply, to act or move in response to

Talk about needing an answer to prayer quickly! It was a disagreeable place to be, and he desired a hasty rescue. Even though his own rebellion against God caused this dilemma, he knew the Lord's help was the only means of escape. Let Jonah tell his story about being swallowed by a great fish.

> From inside the fish Jonah prayed to the Lord his God. He said:
> "In my distress I called to the Lord, and he answered me. From the depths of the grave I called for help and you listened to my cry. You hurled me into the deep, into the very heart of the seas…
> The engulfing waters threatened me, the deep surrounded me; seaweed was wrapped around my head…
> But you brought my life up from the pit, O Lord my God. When my life was ebbing away, I remembered you, Lord, and my prayer rose to you, to your holy temple…"

> And the Lord commanded the fish, and it vomited Jonah onto dry land.
> —JONAH 2:1–3a,5,6b–7,10 NIV

After being rescued from the belly of the fish, Jonah set out to complete the assignment God had given him. His mission was a success, and a whole nation turned to the Lord.

Often we have to suffer the consequences of our own rebellion, but we can still learn valuable lessons. Even if our own sin caused the problem, when we repent and cry out to God, He hears and answers us. The Lord may not always respond in the way or time that we expect, but He always listens as we pray.

> He brought them out of darkness and the shadow of death, and broke their chains in pieces... Those who go down to the sea in ships... see the works of the Lord... They cry out to the Lord in their trouble, and He brings them out of their distresses... He calms the storm... He guides them to their desired haven.
> —PSALM 107:14,23–24,28–30

Here is another amazing contemporary story of God's answer to an urgent request from the battlefield.[1] (The story is from an article in *Guideposts Magazine*, clipped out long ago and given to me.)

It was a clear bright day in March 1945 when soldiers in the U.S. Army Infantry made their way through dense woods in the German Rhineland. Their objective was to reach and capture the town of Ossenburg.

When the soldiers attempted to cross an open field, the enemy fired on them. Three nests of German machine guns were firing at the field, a space of about 200 yards. Crossing the field safely was impossible, yet the men had no choice. All other routes were blocked by Germans.

A desperate young soldier in the group dropped to his knees and asked God to please do something. The order came to move forward. As the young man stepped out of his hiding place in the woods to the edge of the clearing, he glanced to his left and saw a white cloud approaching. It came out of nowhere, moved over the trees, dropped down and covered the field. A thick fog obscured the vision of the enemy soldiers.

The Americans ran across the clearing, and as the last man reached the safety of the nearby woods, the cloud vanished. The infantrymen continued with their mission and succeeded in securing new areas for the Allies.

To further prove to this young man that Divine intervention was at work, he received a letter from home two weeks later telling of prayer offered up for him in the local church. A woman in the congregation was awakened from sleep and ordered by the Lord to pray for that soldier—at the very time he was in mortal danger.

She prayed, "Lord, whatever danger he is in, just cover him with a cloud!"

From that time on, he became a man of steadfast prayer.

> As for me, I will call upon God, and the Lord shall save me. Evening and morning and at noon I will pray, and cry aloud, and He shall hear my voice.
>
> *—PSALM 55:16–17*

Endnotes:

1 *Guideposts Magazine*, P.O. Box 1419, Carmel, NY 10512, from an article by Spenser January. Date of publication unknown.

Chapter 21

Rescued and Honored

I will be with him in trouble; I will deliver him and honor him.

–PSALM 91:15b

Deliver: from the Hebrew word *chalats*, this has the connotation of preparing, strengthening, equipping one to fight a battle. In this definition of *deliver*, one is not taken out of the trouble, but God is with him through it. We must fight, but God equips us.

He was a visionary, a dreamer, and that would lead him on a journey few could imagine. The story of Joseph in the Book of Genesis relates a tale of rejection, betrayal, lies and misunderstanding. Yet it also reveals eventual triumph for this resolute young man.

God planned to use Joseph as His instrument to rescue the Jewish nation from starvation during a time of famine that would later occur. The Lord had to somehow move Joseph to Egypt and transform this spoiled teenager into a disciplined, skilled administrator.

You may recall from Scripture that because Joseph was a favored younger son of Jacob, his older brothers hated him (see Genesis 37:3–4). The older brothers' resentment intensified when seventeen-year-old Joseph told them of a dream he interpreted to mean that someday they would serve him. This was contrary to Jewish custom, since the oldest son inherited the father's authority.

The brothers at first planned to kill Joseph, but instead sold him into slavery. He was taken to Egypt, where he served in the house of Potiphar, Pharaoh's captain of the guard. The young Hebrew found favor with Potiphar, who made him administrator of the household. The Bible says several times that God was with Joseph, and he was successful at whatever he set his hand to.

Just when things seemed to be going well, Joseph was falsely accused of assaulting Potiphar's wife. He spent years in prison. Even there his administrative skills led to a position of leadership.

Eventually released from prison, Joseph interpreted a dream Pharaoh had. Joseph said the dream predicted seven years of plenty in Egypt followed by seven years of famine. Hearing this, Pharaoh appointed Joseph to administer the food supply in preparation for the lean years ahead. Joseph rose from prisoner to Prime Minister, being greatly esteemed by the Egyptians and later by his own family.

He lived to see his own brothers come and bow down to him, as in the dream he had as a teenager. They did not recognize him. With a wave of his hand Joseph could have had his brothers killed, but instead he lavished forgiveness, mercy and love on them (see Genesis 45 and 50:15–21).

Human relationships are the same today; there must be ongoing forgiveness and healing for them to grow stronger.

Joseph went through four stages which often parallel our own journey. Note that we may go through this cycle more than once in a lifetime!

1. First is the challenge. Joseph was sold into slavery by his brothers and taken to a foreign land.

2. Then things seem to improve. Joseph was given favor and authority in Potiphar's house.

3. Just when everything seems to be back on an even keel and going well, our peaceful world comes crashing down. Joseph was falsely accused and thrown into prison.

4. Finally, tribulation is reversed, and we begin to realize our potential, having grown through adversity. Joseph was set free from prison, given favor with Pharaoh, and became Prime Minister of Egypt.

Joseph had to go through some trials, but God was with him through them all. This period of challenge was what God used as a training time. It prepared Joseph for the time, years later, when his skillful administration enabled Egypt and his Jewish family to be preserved during a time of severe drought.

We also can become "bitter or better" through challenging times. With God in control, these can be periods of great spiritual and emotional growth that lead us to a higher plane on our life journey. God promises in Psalm 91:15 that He will be with us in trouble, deliver us and honor us.

We were blessed by the movie *Chariots of Fire*. It tells the story of the 1924 Olympics, in which Scottish missionary Eric Liddell was a competitor.

Liddell was surprised to learn that the 100-meter track event for which he had trained so diligently was scheduled to be held on Sunday. Liddell was strongly committed to Christ and chose to honor the Sabbath instead of participating in the race.

He was severely criticized as his nation's leaders attempted to dissuade him. Despite extreme pressure, Liddell did not compromise his spiritual convictions. He went on to win a gold medal in the 400-meter event later that week and found fame and glory.

After the Olympics, Liddell fulfilled his commitment to be a missionary in China. Like Joseph, he spent some time as a prisoner. Even while incarcerated in China he encouraged fellow prisoners and taught them about trusting God in all things.

God promises to honor those who honor Him (see 1 Samuel 2:30). At Liddell's death, a leading newspaper in his country wrote: "Scotland has lost a son who did her proud every hour of his life."

This tribute was given to Liddell at the end of *Chariots of Fire*: "Eric Liddell, missionary, died in occupied China at the end of World War II. All of Scotland mourned."

...I am not ashamed, for I know (perceive, have knowledge of, and am acquainted with) Him Whom I have believed (adhered to and trusted in and relied on), and I am [positively] persuaded that He is able to guard and keep that which has been entrusted to me and which I have committed [to Him] until that day.
—2 TIMOTHY 1:12 AMP

The first step towards fulfilling our purpose is to understand that there are no insignificant tasks... Those who do great things have greatness in them— not just in their tasks.

If you will do whatever you are doing now with all your heart, if you will face every task with that passion and a devotion to excellence, you will do great things because greatness will be in you. You were made in the image of God who did all things well.

–Rick Joyner

Chapter 22

Long Life and Salvation

With long life I will satisfy him, and show him My salvation.
–Psalm 91:16

Salvation: deliverance, safety, aid, victory, prosperity, welfare; God's saving grace

George Washington, our first President, experienced many instances of Divine intervention on his behalf. During the French and Indian wars, an Indian sprang up from a hiding place and fired at Washington from only three or four paces away. The shots missed him, as did the fifteen bullets another Indian fired at him later.

Providence was at work on another occasion. British Army Major Ferguson was lying in the woods near Philadelphia with his troops, when a horseman unknowingly rode right into their ambush. The Major stepped out of concealment, aimed his rifle, and ordered the tall man in the black hat to stop.

The man stopped, looked at the officer, then rode on. Ferguson aimed right between the shoulder blades of the retreating figure and said he could easily have put four or five bullets in him. But he hated to shoot a man in the back. He later learned that man was George Washington.

Washington's coat had numerous bullet holes in it, but he was never once wounded while he served his country! Washington died at home in Mount Vernon at the age of 67. A throat infection was the cause of death. George Washington was indeed blessed with a long and fruitful life.

> The godly shall flourish like palm trees... For they are transplanted into the Lord's own garden, and are under his personal care. Even in old age they will still produce fruit and be vital and green.
> –PSALM 92:12–14 TLB

Amazing Grace

The word *salvation* has several connotations in addition to spiritual rescue from eternal damnation. We can have the satisfying long life promised in verse 16 as God rescues us physically, mentally and emotionally, as well as spiritually. The Lord promises that we will have the life span needed to accomplish His purpose for our lives.

This book has many stories of rescue from physical danger, but God also saves us from mental and emotional bondage or harmful lifestyles that can destroy our potential.

John Newton, who wrote the hymn "Amazing Grace," was himself a trophy of God's saving grace. Newton was an eighteenth-century slave trader who had little regard for human life. When he came to the Lord, his life changed radically. John lived to a ripe old age, and when asked at age 82 when he would retire, he said, "Never!"

> Though I am not what I ought to be, or hope to be, I can truly say I am not what I once was... By the grace of God, I am what I am!
> –John Newton

Bill Wilson, founder of Alcoholics Anonymous, had a life-changing experience when he sought God for help as he lay dying of alcohol-related sickness. At death's door, he was desperate to live and cried out, "If there is a God, show me, show me. Give me some sign."[1]

As told by Robert Thomsen in his book *Bill W.*, at that moment, Wilson became aware of a great white light that filled his room. He was caught up in a great joy, an indescribable ecstasy. He seemed to be standing on a mountaintop with a strong, clear wind of the Spirit blowing around and through him. He was aware of a Presence, which made him feel complete and satisfied for the first time in his life.

When the experience was over, Bill was filled with a peace that he had never before known. He no longer felt lost, alone and hopeless, and became certain of a Divine order in the universe. He was set free of alcoholism and went on to found AA, an organization which has changed countless lives.

> For we are God's [own] handiwork (His workmanship), recreated in Christ Jesus, [born anew] that we may do those good works which God predestined (planned beforehand) for us [taking paths which He prepared ahead of time], that we should walk in them [living the good life which He prearranged and made ready for us to live].
> –*EPHESIANS 2:10* AMP

Endnotes:

1 Robert Thomsen, *Bill W*, Perennial Library, 1975.

Amazing Grace

Amazing Grace how sweet the sound
That saved a wretch like me
I once was lost, but now am found
Was blind but now I see

'Twas grace that taught my heart to fear
And grace my fears relieved
How precious did that grace appear
The hour I first believed

The Lord has promised good to me
His word my hope secures
He will my shield and portion be
As long as life endures

Through many dangers toils and snares
I have already come
'Tis grace has brought me safe thus far
And grace will lead me home.

–John Newton

God is able to make all grace abound toward you, that you… may have an abundance for every good work.

–2 Corinthians 9:8

Chapter 23

Never a Problem?

"In the world you will have tribulation; but be of good cheer, I have overcome the world."
—*JOHN 16:33b*

Problem: a situation that presents uncertainty, difficulty, perplexity or trouble

They had done everything required, being exemplary young men. Yet here they were, about to get into a really hot spot. Meshach, Shadrack and Abed-Nego obeyed the king faithfully until he commanded them to bow down and worship false gods. They refused to abandon the One True God.

The king's ultimatum was to obey or be cast into a fiery furnace. They knew the character of their Lord, and proclaimed boldly, "If that is the case, our God whom we serve is able to deliver us from the burning fiery furnace..." (see Daniel 3:17).

The Book of Daniel tells how they were thrown into the red hot furnace, but God was with them to deliver them. When the king looked into the furnace, he saw the three walking in the flames, and a fourth person—"who looks like the Son of God"—in the fire with them. (Scholars believe this fourth person in the fire with them was the pre-incarnate Jesus.) When the king released the young men, even their hair and clothing were unsinged! The only thing that burned were the ropes that bound them.

Sometimes fiery trials serve to burn away the things that bind us.

It is important to know that one does not escape every problem. We must go through some difficulties to strengthen and perfect us, but we can be certain that God is with us in any trial, as He was with these saints:

- Noah had to spend time on the ark with lots of noisy (and probably smelly) animals before he was free to roam (see Genesis 7, 8).
- Moses and the Israelites wandered in the desert for forty years before they came to the Promised Land (see Exodus 13 and following).
- David, who had already been anointed king of Israel, spent time on the run and in a cave hiding from King Saul before he assumed the throne (see 1 Samuel 16 to 2 Samuel 5).
- Paul the Apostle was beaten, persecuted and imprisoned for the Gospel, yet kept his joy and purpose (see 2 Corinthians 4:8–10).

How can you have victory if you've never been in a battle?

The story of World War II flying ace Captain Eddie Rickenbacker has given hope to many who find themselves in challenging circumstances.

On October 21, 1942, a B-17 Flying Fortress crashed into the Pacific. The five-man crew and their three passengers, among them Captain Eddie Rickenbacker, managed to escape the plane and climb aboard life rafts. Their only equipment was a sheath knife, two sets of oars, a few fish hooks and a line snatched from a parachute.

They had no water or food except for four oranges. All night long the men shivered in the rafts, which were being circled by sharks. As the second night approached, there was no sign of rescue planes, and the survivors were desperately thirsty. Several of the men prayed regularly, believing for God's Divine intervention. Their hope began to fade as they consumed the last orange on their fourth day afloat.

When their hunger was agonizing, and their spirits at the lowest ebb, a sea swallow appeared out of nowhere and landed on Captain Rickenbacker's head. They caught the bird and ate its raw flesh. They used the bird's intestines for bait and caught several small fish for food. Though this meager meal decreased their hunger, it increased their thirst.

They continued to read from a small Bible one man had, coming upon Matthew 6:31–34. Here Jesus instructs us not to worry about what we will eat or drink, because Father God knows what we need.

A crew member prayed for continued supply. On the sixth night they fired a flare to attract a rescue plane. It fizzled and fell into the sea. Yet this discouraging event turned advantageous when the flare's light attracted a school of good sized fish. Two of the fish jumped right into one of the rafts!

During their prayer time on the eighth evening, drinking water was their main request, since they probably could not survive much longer without it. Before long a cloud appeared and soon deluged the men with sheets of drinkable water. On the eleventh day another cloud deluged them with more.

Their trials continued for days, even to having a rescue plane pass them by, and a crew member die. Finally after twenty-one days they were rescued.

These men were not kept from tribulation, yet God was with them throughout repeated attacks and did eventually rescue them. The survivors' lives were changed dramatically, including finding faith in the Lord and belief in His provision.

Even when things all around you seem bleak and hopeless, never give up. God will deliver you!

> The eyes of the Lord are on the righteous and his ears are attentive to their cry...
> The righteous cry out, and the Lord hears them; He delivers them from all their troubles...
> The Lord is close to the brokenhearted and saves those who are crushed in spirit.
> A righteous man may have many troubles, but the Lord delivers him from them all.
> —PSALM 34:15,17–19 NIV

Don't Quit

When things go wrong as they sometimes will,
When the road you're trudging seems all uphill,
When the funds are low, and the debts are high,
And you want to smile, but you have to sigh,
When care is pressing you down a bit,
Rest if you must, but don't you quit.

Life is queer with its twists and turns,
As every one of us sometimes learns,
And many a failure turns about,
When he might have won had he stuck it out.
Don't give up though the pace seems slow;
You may succeed with another blow.

Success is failure turned inside out,
The silver tint in the clouds of doubt.
And you never can tell how close you are;
It may be near when it seems so far.
So stick to the fight when you're hardest hit,
It's when things seem worst
That you must not quit.

–Kirstone

Chapter 24

A Friend of God

The Lord spoke to Moses face to face, as a man speaks to his friend... [God said,] "I will also do this thing that you have spoken; for you have found grace in My sight, and I know you by name."
−*EXODUS 33:11,17*

"No longer do I [Jesus] call you servants... but I have called you friends..."
−*JOHN 15:15*

Friend: a person whom one knows, likes and trusts; a favored companion

Uncle Mike opened a whole new world to our eight-year-old granddaughter Jordyn when he gave her a microscope for Christmas. She was amazed to see a drop of pond water changed through magnification into a pool teeming with life. Tiny creatures and plants she never knew existed appeared through the microscope lens. Leaves, a strand of hair and other everyday objects were transformed under the power of magnification.

Delightedly, Jordyn said, "Wow! There are a whole bunch of things I never knew were there! Things sure look different when I see them under the microscope."

At that moment the Lord spoke to my heart and drew a parallel to our relationship with Him. He seemed to say, "Many of you have been walking with Me for years, yet know little about the depth of My Being. You see surface things and think that's all there is. But I long to show you so much more."

That is the cry of His heart to all of us. God beckons us to commune with Him. He wants us to have friendship with Him. He says,

> "Behold, I stand at the door and knock. If anyone hears My voice and opens the door, I will come in to him and dine with him, and he with Me."
> —REVELATION 3:20

Relationship Versus Fellowship

A local pastor spoke recently on the concept of walking intimately with God after we have committed our hearts to Him. He gave the example of being closely related to his earthly father, something that will never change. Even if he rarely talks with his dad, there is still a blood connection. In the same way, after we have made Christ our Savior, we have a relationship with Him established by the blood He shed on the cross.

Intimate fellowship is another matter. When we spend time sharing with a loved one or a dear friend, a closeness develops. Communion with God is like that. Choosing to dwell in the secret place with Him leads to a depth of intimacy that goes beyond simple relationship. One teacher defined the secret place as "a place where God tells you His secrets" (see Psalm 25:14).

Just think of it: God the Almighty, Kings of Kings, Majestic Creator of the universe, longs to have fellowship with *you*! You are so precious to Him that He wants to spend time with you, walk and talk with you, develop a close friendship with you and reveal His nature to you (see Psalm 147:11).

How can we have the faith and trust to believe that God will protect and provide for us as He did for those mentioned in earlier chapters? How can we be confident that His love will uphold us no matter how dire the circumstances seem to be, no matter how dangerous, hopeless, unending the situation is? How can we find the eye in the midst of the storm?

The assurance of the Lord's faithfulness is gained by a revelation of who He is. This is imparted through an intimacy with God that causes us to know for certain that He will never leave or forsake us.

How can we experience this? By spending time in the secret place alone with God, communing with and waiting silently before Him. In human relationships, it is necessary to regularly be with one whom we seek to know well. In courtship, we get to know our beloved as we spend hours talking with and listening to him. And that also is the key to intimate friendship with the Almighty!

George Mueller knew the secret of unwavering faith and trust. He was a nineteenth-century preacher who was completely surrendered to God's will and in continual communion with Him.

Mueller set out to show unbelievers in Britain that God was still in control. Without ever expressing a need to anyone, going only to God in prayer with his requests, Mueller changed a nation. He set up schools to teach adults and children to read and write. He supported missionaries throughout the world. The Lord gave him a burden for orphans at a time when only those with wealthy relatives could go to orphanages. As told in Charles Dickens' stories, most orphans in England had a very difficult life. Many were thrown in prison to keep them off the streets.

After ascertaining that planning to build the orphanage in Bristol, England, was indeed the Lord's will, Mueller asked God to provide a house, caregivers, a certain sum of money, furniture and clothing for the children who would come. He said he had no natural prospect of obtaining these things, but it was not too difficult for his heavenly Father to grant.

After these things were sovereignly provided and the home established, there were times when desperate needs arose. On some days there was no food at all, and no money. Yet God always came through, using various people and unusual means, sometimes at the last minute.

Not once did Mueller ever express a financial need to anyone. His faith in his beloved Lord never wavered, and God always provided for him and the children.

This message of trust in a father's loving care was illustrated to me recently when our family vacationed together at a lake. Our sixteen-month-old granddaughter was in water with her father, floating on a raft.

A concerned family member asked the child's mother, "Aren't you afraid to have the baby out there?"

Our daughter replied, "Why should I worry? She's in her father's arms!"

In the same way, we can be secure in our heavenly Father's arms, knowing that He will not allow anything to come our way without His permission. Once we have established that intimate relationship with Him, we will have complete trust in His love for us and all that love encompasses.

> I know whom I have believed and am persuaded that He is able to keep what I have committed to Him until that Day.
> –2 TIMOTHY 1:12

Why would one be content to stand in the doorway when he is invited to dwell in the King's presence and share all He has to give?

—*Andrew Murray*

Chapter 25

Keys to the Secret Place

> The secret [of the sweet, satisfying companionship] of the Lord have they who fear (revere and worship) Him, and He will show them His covenant and reveal to them its [deep, inner] meaning.
> —PSALM 25:14 AMP

Key: a means of entry or possession

God is the one who births in us a desire for intimacy with Him. There seems to be a great hunger among believers today to draw nearer to the Lord. He delights in our quest and wants to lead us into a closer relationship with Him.

Scripture says God's friend Moses knew His ways, whereas the Israelites only knew His deeds, that is, what they could see with their natural eyes (see Psalm 103:7). God wants to take us beyond the level of surface acquaintance, into a realm of deeper knowledge of Him and His ways. Following are some suggestions on how to develop an intimate relationship with the God of all creation.

Keys to the Secret Place

> In everything you do, put God first, and he will direct you and crown your efforts with success.
> —*Proverbs 3:6 TLB*

As said previously, the most important step is to make Jesus the Lord of your life.

Spend time with Him—quality and quantity time. If Jesus often went to a quiet place to commune with His Father, how much more should we!

Set aside a daily time to be with God. Consistency is key. If necessary, mark it as an appointment on your schedule.

How can you get to know someone well if you seldom speak with him? The same is true of the relationship with God. *Daily* communion with Him, abiding on a *continual* basis, causes us to increasingly know Him, His character and the way He thinks. Then we will be able to hear when He speaks and discern whether a thing is from Him or from other sources. Jesus said that His sheep follow Him because they know His voice and will not follow a stranger (see John 10:4–5).

If you find it difficult to just sit, play worship music softly in the background and meditate on a portion of Scripture. Ask God to help you in this quest.

Sanctify a place. Moses went to the tent of meeting to seek God's presence (see Exodus 33:9). Jesus went alone to a quiet place to pray (see Luke 5:16). The space where you meet with God can be a prayer room set aside for that purpose, a kitchen table, or wherever else you meet with Him daily.

When my sister Jean had three small children, including infant twin boys, she would go into the bathroom after dinner and lock the door to be alone with God for a set period of time. Her husband watched the youngsters and allowed no interruptions to interfere with that short time Jean had with the Lord.

Renew your mind with God's Word (see Romans 12:2). When you study the Bible, you'll learn of His many promises. You can use them to refute fear, wild imaginations, and words of doom spoken over you.

Praise and worship the Lord during that time with Him. Scripture says to enter His gates with thanksgiving and His courts with praise (see Psalm 100:4). Praise brings God on the scene, as verified in Psalm 22:3, which promises that the Lord inhabits the praises of His people.

Develop a friendship with the Holy Spirit. He is our teacher and counselor (see John 14:26). God The Holy Spirit has a key role in leading us into relationship with God the Father and God the Son. Reverend Mike Bickle says, "…what the Holy Spirit enjoys most and does best is to escort the heart of the spiritually hungry into a realm of experiential knowledge of the splendor of Jesus."[1]

Be willing, obedient and thankful. In Matthew 26:41 Jesus admits that "the spirit is willing, but the flesh is weak." Take daily steps to discipline your flesh, mind and spirit. Form the habit of immediate obedience to the Lord's direction. The Old Testament tells us:

> If you are willing and obedient, you shall eat the good of the land.
> –ISAIAH 1:19

These are the words of Jesus from the New Testament:

> "If anyone loves Me, he will obey my teaching. My Father will love him, and We will come to him and make Our home with him."
> –JOHN 14:23

Become childlike (not childish). Develop an open heart.

A friend who has a Ph.D. recently came into this joyful knowledge of intimacy with God and said that his intellect and reasoning previously interfered with experiencing the Lord's acceptance and closeness. God delights when we use our intellect for His glory, but there are times when continuous questioning, reasoning, and using scientific theories can get in the way of simple childlike faith.

Keep a journal of victories, answered prayers, triumphs over circumstances. You may be surprised at how mature, wise and courageous you've become.

Be available. I desire to speak regularly with my daughter who lives a thousand miles from me, so I need to be available when she calls. If I am not there to answer the phone, no communication can take place. Likewise, we must have a receptive spirit and a mindset open to the Lord, so that God can get through anywhere, any time. Don't let Him continually get a busy signal when He tries to speak with you.

Be patient. Relationships in both the natural and spiritual realms take time to develop. Just as fruit in a garden takes time to mature, our walk with the Lord is a growing process. *Consistent daily fellowship* is the key ingredient to nourishing that friendship with God.

God loves you, knows you intimately, and calls you by name. As you develop a closeness to Him, and a knowledge of His character, you will gain confidence that your Friend will always be there for you. You'll know for certain that God will protect, guide and provide, and fulfill His promises to you, including those in Psalm 91.

In my own life, there have been numerous blessings from abiding in the Lord. Early in my Christian walk it was interesting to discover that even new Christians can have close communion with God and be His conduit to help others.

Twenty years ago, newly born again, I had a childlike dependence on and faith in God's providential care. I had Myasthenia Gravis, a muscle disease, and could only get along in His strength.

About a year into my journey with Christ, I felt God directing me to join my neighbor in taking a refresher nursing course at a local hospital. We spent a short time in each hospital department, updating our knowledge and skills.

On the day we were scheduled to work in the emergency room, my fellow student Marilyn and I were asked to take care of Sam. He was a forty-eight-year-old alcoholic who lived on the streets of Baltimore. He was in despair and had laid down in the snow to die. When the paramedics brought him in, his prognosis was poor. Death seemed imminent.

Sickness, despair, and the alcohol in his system caused Sam to speak loudly and disparagingly. He reeked of alcohol and body odor, apparently not having bathed in some time.

In the next bed, separated only by a thin curtain, lay a six-year-old boy who needed sutures to close a cut near his eye. The head nurse asked us to stay with Sam and try to quiet him so the child would not be fearful and restless during the suturing process.

That morning before work I had spent time with God, making myself available to serve Him in whatever capacity He chose. This assignment was not exactly what I had in mind, but I had learned to trust His plans and purposes in my life.

Sam had evidently heard sermons at the Salvation Army and from various street preachers over the years, and he loudly quoted Bible passages about God's wrath. I had only been reading the Bible for about a year and was astonished to hear myself respond to each negative verse about judgment with one about God's love and care.

Out of my mouth came scriptural answers I didn't even realize I knew. Within a short time Sam quieted down and told me he had known the Lord at one time, but had walked away from God after a series of heartaches. He had been an alcoholic living on the streets for twenty-four of his forty-eight years, and the future seemed hopeless.

As I reflected on all this later on, I realized that Sam had become sober and rational very quickly during our conversation and the offensive odor seemed almost to be replaced by a light sweet fragrance. Surprisingly, there seemed to be no thought in my mind about others around us listening in—it's almost as if we were transported to another place.

The Lord spoke through me that He loved Sam very much and was able to heal him and give him a new life.

Sam's pale blue eyes searched mine as he said, "Do you really think that is possible?"

Since God had done so much in my life, I could say with absolute certainty, "Sam, I *know* it is."

The three of us prayed a prayer of recommitment to Christ and asked that God would heal and restore. Shortly after that Marilyn and I had to leave to attend classes.

At the end of the day, Marilyn called me aside and tearfully shared that she too had walked away from God several years ago, devastated when her young son developed a chronic illness.

"I know He has been calling me back," she said, "but I was really angry with Him. Yet something happened when we prayed with Sam this morning. I felt such a sense of God's presence and love, and have peace and hope for the first time in ages."

What an unexpected bonus from the One whose presence made it all happen!

The next day I called the hospital admitting office to see what room Sam was in, preparing to visit him.

The clerk said, "We have no record of an admission; he probably passed away."

I stopped by the emergency room to get more details and was surprised at the response: "Oh, no, he didn't die, though we expected him to. To everyone's amazement, he quickly got much better and was able to walk out of here apparently recovered! Beside that, today he came in to see a counselor and signed up for an alcohol rehabilitation program."

Now it was my turn for tears, tears of joy at the Lord's faithfulness. As a postscript, I met Marilyn a year later and she said her son was close to full recovery. Several years after that, God totally healed me of "incurable" Myasthenia Gravis!

Recalling that long ago experience, I am still awed by how the Lord gave each of us what we needed that day. A suicidal alcoholic, a young mom who had succumbed to self-pity and bitterness, and a nurse who needed to look at God's healing promises rather than medical prognoses... all of us were met personally by the Creator that day and showered with His overwhelming love.

God is the same yesterday, today and forever. He stands with *you* at this very moment, prepared to pour out that same blessing.

Right here, right now, soak in His presence. Drink deeply of the life-giving water, breathe in His sweet fragrance and receive all He has to give. Your life will never be the same!

> The Lord your God is in the midst of you, a Mighty One, a Savior [Who saves]! He will rejoice over you with joy; He will rest [in silent satisfaction] and in His love He will be silent and make no mention [of past sins, or even recall them]; He will exult over you with singing.
> —ZEPHANIAH 3:17 AMP

Endnotes:

1 Mike Bickle, "Fascinated By God," *Charisma Magazine*, December 1999.

Prayers of Blessing

The earnest (heartfelt, continued) prayer of a righteous man makes tremendous power available [dynamic in its working].
–JAMES 5:16b AMP

Praying God's word over a person is very significant. The Lord says that His word is living and powerful (see Hebrews 4:12). God promises us that:

So shall My word be that goes forth from My mouth; it shall not return to Me void, but it shall accomplish what I please, and it shall prosper in the thing for which I sent it.
–ISAIAH 55:11

With those promises in mind, following are two prayers for you and your loved ones.

Prayer of Blessing from Psalm 91

May you dwell in the secret place of the most high,
And abide under the shadow of the Almighty.
May you trust in the Lord and know that He is your refuge and fortress.
May God deliver you from snares and pestilence.
May He hide you under His wings and be your shield.
May you have no fear of attacks night or day.

Even if people all around you fall, may trouble not come near you.
May you make the Lord Most High your refuge and dwelling place.
May God's angels keep you in all your ways.
May you know you have the power to trample evil underfoot.
As you set your love on God, may He deliver you and set you on high.
May He answer your prayers, be with you in trouble and honor you.
May the Lord satisfy you with a long life and with salvation.

Prayer of Blessing from Ephesians 1 and 3

I pray for you constantly, asking God… to give you wisdom to see clearly and really understand who Christ is and all that He has done for you.

I pray that your hearts will be flooded with light so that you can see something of the future He has called you to share…

I pray that you will begin to understand how incredibly great His power is to help those who believe in Him…

I pray that Christ will be more and more at home in your hearts, living within you as you trust Him.

May your roots go down deep into the soil of God's marvelous love; and may you be able to feel and understand… how long, how wide, how deep and how high His love really is; and to experience this love for yourselves… so at last you will be filled up with God Himself!

–EPHESIANS 1:16–19; 3:17–19 TLB

Appendix

Promises from Scripture

God Gives Victory

He [God] holds victory in store for the upright, he is a shield for those whose walk is blameless, for he guards the course of the just and protects the way of his faithful ones.
—*PROVERBS 2:7–8 NIV*

The Lord knows how to rescue the godly.
—*2 PETER 2:9 AMP*

Now thanks be to God who always leads us in triumph in Christ.
—*2 CORINTHIANS 2:14a*

Be not afraid of sudden terror and panic, nor of the stormy blast or the storm and ruin of the wicked when it comes [for you will be guiltless], for the Lord shall be your confidence, firm and strong, and shall keep your foot from being caught [in a trap or hidden danger].
—*PROVERBS 3:25–26 AMP*

People who know their God shall be strong, and carry out great exploits.
—*DANIEL 11:32b*

God's Promises to Combat Fear

For God has not given us a spirit of fear, but of power and of love and of a sound mind.
—2 Timothy 1:7

Fear not, for I am with you.
—Isaiah 43:5

[The Lord says]... Don't be afraid, for I have ransomed you; I have called you by name; you are mine. When you go through deep waters and trouble, I will be with you. When you go through rivers of difficulty, you will not drown! When you walk through the fire of oppression, you will not be burned up—the flames will not consume you. For I am the Lord your God, your Savior...
—Isaiah 43:1–3a TLB

I will fear no evil, for you are with me...
—Psalm 23:4b NIV

You need not be afraid of sudden disaster... for the Lord is with you. He protects you.
—Proverbs 3:25

He [God] shall give His angels charge over you, to keep you in all your ways.
—Psalm 91:11

Be strong and courageous. Do not be terrified; do not be discouraged, for the Lord your God will be with you wherever you go.
—Joshua 1:9 NIV

Do not fear, for I am with you; do not be dismayed, for I am your God. I will strengthen you and help you; I will uphold you with My righteous right hand.
—ISAIAH 41:10 NIV

Do not fear... The Lord your God is with you, he is mighty to save. He will take great delight in you, he will quiet you with his love, he will rejoice over you with singing.
—ZEPHANIAH 3:16–17 NIV

God's Promises for Provision

My God will meet all your needs according to his glorious riches in Christ Jesus.
—PHILIPPIANS 4:19 NIV

"Consider the ravens: they do not sow or reap, they have no storeroom or barn; yet God feeds them. And how much more valuable are you than birds!"
—LUKE 12:24 NIV

I was young and now I am old, yet I have never seen the righteous forsaken or their children begging bread.
—PSALM 37:25 NIV

No good thing will He withhold from those who walk uprightly.
—PSALM 84:11b

[You are] like a tree planted by streams of water, which yields its fruit in season and whose leaf does not wither. Whatever [you do] prospers.
—PSALM 1:3 NIV

"If… God clothes the grass, which is here today, and tomorrow is thrown into the fire, how much more will He clothe you…"
—LUKE 12:28 NIV

"Do not fear, little flock, for it is the Father's good pleasure to give you the kingdom."
—LUKE 12:32

Blessed is the man who fears the Lord, who finds great delight in his commands… He will have no fear of bad news; his heart is steadfast, trusting in the Lord. His heart is secure, he will have no fear.
—PSALM 112:1b,7–8 NIV

The Lord will perfect that which concerns me.
—PSALM 138:8

God Gives Hope

Now thanks be to God who always leads us in triumph in Christ…
—2 CORINTHIANS 2:14a

When the enemy comes in like a flood, the Spirit of the Lord will lift up a standard against him.
—ISAIAH 59:19b

The Lord is close to the brokenhearted and saves those who are crushed in spirit. A righteous man may have many troubles, but the LORD delivers him from them all;
—PSALM 34:18–19 NIV

The eternal God is your refuge, and underneath are the everlasting arms.
—DEUTERONOMY 33:27

I know in whom I have believed, and I am convinced that he is able to guard what I have entrusted to him for that day.
—2 TIMOTHY 1:12 NIV

God Gives Peace of Mind

You will guard him and keep him in perfect and constant peace whose mind [both its inclination and its character] is stayed on You, because he commits himself to You, leans on You, and hopes confidently in You.
—ISAIAH 26:3 AMP

"Peace I leave you; My [own] peace I now give and bequeath to you. Not as the world gives do I give to you. Do not let your heart be troubled, neither let it be afraid."
—JOHN 14:27 AMP

You will go out in joy and be led forth in peace.
—ISAIAH 55:12 NIV

In peace I will both lie down and sleep, for You, Lord, alone make me dwell in safety and confident trust.
—PSALM 4:8 AMP

And the peace of God, which surpasses all understanding, shall keep your hearts and minds through Christ Jesus.
—PHILIPPIANS 4:7

About the Author

Camille Nehmsmann, a registered nurse, received her diploma from St. Peter's School of Nursing in New Brunswick, New Jersey, and her degree in school nursing from Glassboro State College, now called Rowan College, in Glassboro, New Jersey. She worked briefly in hospital nursing before her children were born.

Camille received Christ into her heart in 1977 and since then has participated in a number of intercessory prayer groups and taught on the power of intercessory prayer. She has also led home fellowship groups and been active in women's ministries.

Camille has written three other books whose purpose is to lead people into a closer walk with the Lord.

Camille and her husband Lou have been married forty years. They have three children and three grandchildren. They presently reside in Washington Township, Pennsylvania.

For book covers or custom artwork, contact:

Kathy Kinaites
813 Bellus Road
Hinckley, OH 44233

To produce a book such as this one, contact:

Howard Professional Services
1111 Summitt Street
White Oak, PA 15131

Additional copies of this book are available from:

Good News Ministries
301 Young Drive
Apollo, PA 15613

Also available from Camille Nehmsmann:

Meet The God Who Loves You, a gentle evangelistic message for those who need to hear how God can make a difference in their lives. Written in simple, easily understood language, this book is filled with encouraging stories that also give hope to believers, whatever their stage of growth.

Discover Hidden Treasure, a brief summary of every book of the Bible, including a chronology of the Old Testament and historical background to biblical events. Written in easy to understand language with encouraging promises from God's Word.

The Power of Intercessory Prayer, a simple step-by-step guide to intercession, including faith-building stories of dramatic answers to prayer. Some of the topics discussed in this book are spiritual warfare, the importance of praise, Scripture praying, interceding for the unsaved, and group prayer.

Camille Nehmsmann
301 Yound Drive
Apollo, Pa. 15613

Safe In The Secret Place -------------- $8.95
                                                  3 for $25.00
Meet The God Who Loves You ----- $6.95
Discover Hidden Treasure ----------- $5.95
The Power of Intercessory Prayer -$6.95

20% discount for orders of 20 or more

Add $1.75 for postage for the first book,
and 50 cents postage for each additional book.

Make checks payable to Camille Nehmsmann

Book Title	Number of Copies	Price
----------	----------	----------
----------	----------	----------
----------	----------	----------
----------	Postage	----------
	Total	----------

Mail to: (Please Print Clearly)

Name:_____

Address:_____

City:_____

State:_____Zip:_____